$\mathcal{S}^{\text{A}}$ PIRITUAL JOURNEY

An Irishman learns how to embrace life's challenges
to find inner strength and enlightenment

SEAN BOYLAN

Printed in the United States of America.

Library of Congress Control Number: 2020901496

| ISBN | Paperback | 978-1-64361-913-2 |
| | eBook | 978-1-64361-914-9 |

Westwood Books Publishing LLC
11416 SW Aventino Drive
Port Saint Lucie, FL 34987

www.westwoodbookspublishing.com

To those who influenced me and helped with this book…

Thank you to my dear ancestors, who had such a positive influence on my early life.

Thanks to my immediate family for their unwavering support – my brother, three sisters and two wonderful sons; it means everything to me.

A special thank you to my ever-loving wife, whose support and unconditional love is inspiring.

Thanks to my publishers, Westwood Books Publishing in the US, who had the foresight to persuade me to-republish with them and who have supported me with everything.

Finally, a thank you to Warrenpoint writer and poet, Marion Clarke, whose expertise and edits helped my manuscript to flow. She has added her heart to my book.

To those I once believed caused me harm, I dedicate this book – without my ordeal, 'A Spiritual Journey' might never have been written.

CONTENTS

INTRODUCTION

So far, my life on this earth has been full, eventful and challenging. Sometimes it has been all of these at once, when I have been faced with difficult emotional and financial obstacles. The burden of such stresses could have left me a husk of my former self, but by reaching out to the universe and embracing the power of love, I have experienced significant spiritual development and attained a previously unknown level of light and inner peace in my life. It is how this enlightenment came about that I wish to share with you in *A Spiritual Journey.*

As humans on this earth, we all have this potential within us; sometimes we just need a little help to realise it. I hope that this book will encourage you to take stock of your life in a positive way, so you too can see how every stage of life to date is significant, contributing to your knowledge and spirituality, regardless of whether or not you practise a religion. The most important thing for us to learn is how to live our lives to the fullest of our potential because, in doing so, we come to realise that we are much more than this temporal body and are *all* part of the bigger picture on this earth. In other words, we have no limits and we are not alone.

In the telling of this story, I open my heart in a way that I never thought possible. In fact, a few short years ago, I could not have written this book so, in its pages, I have been totally honest. As a result of this voyage and, more importantly, as a result of the challenges and difficulties I have faced, I have become increasingly open and now worry a lot less about what people think of me. I have purposely stripped away most of my ego and misguided opinions about myself and, instead, strive to be the most authentic and loving person that I can be in order to fulfil my life's purpose here on earth. This has been, and continues to be, an incredibly liberating exercise.

Mine is a journey that began in Ireland, where I grew up during The Troubles, and took me to the far side of Europe many times, to Bulgaria, which I experienced both as a communist country and democratic republic. It is difficult to express the extent to which this country has contributed to my growth as a person. My journey also took me to Turkey, where I had a major spiritual experience. Finally, perhaps the most significant change in me as a person, as well as in my spiritual growth, was brought about by the immense challenges I faced in more recent times in my business life in Ireland. These would eventually serve to bring me to a much higher spiritual level.

My sincere wish is that my story in *A Spiritual Journey* will encourage you to open your heart as I have done, so that you too may achieve such enlightenment.

Photograph of the author, Sean Boylan

As a professional photographer, I always found nature inspirational as a subject, and believe that immersing ourselves in our natural surroundings is healing for both body and mind. I will therefore share some of my nature photography with you through the pages of *A Spiritual Journey*.

CHAPTER 1

BEGINNINGS

I was born in County Monaghan, Ireland, in a small parish located almost on the border between Northern Ireland and the Republic. Tyholland straddles the counties of Monaghan and Armagh, which meant that I lived three kilometres (just under two miles) from the United Kingdom, since the six counties of Northern Ireland were, and still are, under its jurisdiction.

I was the youngest of a family of seven children – three boys and four girls. However, like many families, ours was not without its share of misfortune and we were devastated when my eldest brother died tragically (I write about this life-changing event later) Also, within just three days of having the first symptoms, one of my sisters died from a brain tumour. When she was still on a life support system in the hospital, I knew instinctively that she had passed, even though at that stage she was being kept "alive" by the machine that provided artificial respiration.

I often had spiritual "feelings" when I was growing up and felt different to the other members of my family, as I seemed to be on another plain from them, or almost from a different generation. However, all of my family members have always been very considerate and understanding towards me.

When I was in my early teens, sometimes I had the urge to pray in a completely different way to that which I had been taught, or witnessed, within the Catholic community of my parish. I felt that something or someone was guiding me to go outside the house and lie, face-down, on the ground in order to pray or meditate. This was completely new to me and I didn't understand it, but I felt driven to do it. Also, when praying with the family, I found I was unable to recite the words of the prayers we had been taught at home and at school. However. I discovered that if I spoke very slowly I was able to feel the words and this seemed to work, even though it made me different to the others. I remember that my brother used to look at me strangely, no doubt wondering what on earth I was doing!

Our family was not very well off, so there was never any spare cash back in those days. I know that my mother often relied on my uncle to give her money for the weekly groceries, as my father, who was in partnership with him, was not very active in the family business. My mother used to tell us that our uncle had no idea about the cost of buying food for a family of nine. Often she would send me on my bicycle across the border to the shops in the North, where I could buy groceries such as butter and flour at a cheaper price. I had to pass a Northern Irish police checkpoint and separate Customs Post, but those on duty didn't pass much remarks on me or my siblings as we went back and forth across the border with our bags of "illicit" purchases.

Although I never understood exactly what troubled my father, I know that he suffered with some type of nervous condition or form of depression. This meant he couldn't interact with the public and only left the house when he was required to walk around the employees to check work in progress in the family business. The "concrete works" manufactured roofing tiles and concrete water pipes for natural wells and drainage. In fact, thinking about it, I don't remember much about my father before he became ill, but I know he was still a gentle, caring father, despite how terrible he must have been feeling inside.

The concrete business was founded by my father and his brother in the early 1920s, when he was well and full of life, in the days after Southern Ireland gained independence from the UK. My mother, who was very religious and spiritual, was also open-minded, and after she passed over she become one of my spirit guides, as did my father and my brother who died tragically.

Having been brought up as a Catholic in a religious household, we were of course taught how to say lots of prayers. However, as I have already mentioned, I found this particularly difficult as I felt that I couldn't just recite words like that, parrot fashion. Even in my early teens I always had to feel something as I prayed, so that it had some meaning for me.

The family gift of divining

My father and my uncle Hughie had the gift of "divining", or locating spring water underground using a divining rod. I used to travel with my uncle to country farmhouses around Monaghan and further afield to find spring wells for the owners of the property, so that they would know where to find fresh drinking water for their homes.

I was in awe of my Uncle Hughie, as a great amount of self-belief must have been required to undertake this process, since the owners of the land had to commit to digging. The wells were sometimes very deep and the process meant relying on hope, faith and a lot of hard work. There was a great lesson in all this for me, as I was able to acquire these qualities for myself, and soon realised I could also do this by holding the divining rod, just as Hughie had done.

I would hold the Y-shaped stick with both hands and wait for it to receive the energy from any underground water below. When located, the stick would swing, with great force, to point to the spot where the spring water was located underground. I would often find the power of the spring's energy so great that it was often impossible to stop the stick moving, which could have been up to thirty metres beneath my feet. I have always been honoured to have inherited this skill from my father and his brother.

I was to later learn that my father was a very progressive man.

Stream near my home. Picture by the author

My father saves Adolf from Adolf

I learned that in the 1920s, my father, James Boylan, travelled to Germany to purchase machinery for the manufacture of concrete products, such as roofing tiles, that were increasingly required for the new houses that were being built around Monaghan and beyond. At the time, this was a huge step for a small farming family living in a rural location such as Tyholland which was right on the border. In fact, this very same border between Europe and Northern Ireland, and hence the United Kingdom, looks likely to take on a much greater role with recent political events.

Anyway, after purchasing the machinery in Germany, my father made friends with the owner of the factory, Adolf Meinheim, who was a German Jew. Of course, prior to World War II, the Germans had already begun to persecute the Jews and those who were in business were in a very precarious situation. When Adolf sent a desperate message to our house asking my father to save him from the Nazis, my father responded by issuing an urgent invitation through the Irish Department of Foreign Affairs inviting Adolf to come to Monaghan to live with us. He received an immediate response to enter Ireland on the strength of my father's invitation. In fact, my father and my uncle built an ensuite room for him at my uncle's house, which was next to our house. In my youth, years after the end of the war, there were constant references to Adolf as he had become part of our family. He ended up staying many years in Ireland and his brother also came to visit. After the war, our German 'father' Adolf returned to Germany and I have a copy of a postcard he sent from Baden-Baden, so I presume this is where he died. I intend to travel there to visit his grave one day.

When I realised that my father had effectively saved Adolf's life, it had a massive emotional effect on me – in a good way, of course. In return for the kindness and love he received from our family, he gave us so much love back. This is a great lesson for us all, that if we are "flathulach"* with our love, we will get an unlimited amount of love in return.

I had an encounter with a young Jewish man once, while waiting at Gatwick Airport in London for one of my flights to Bulgaria. I told him the story of Adolf and was very surprised when he told me that my father and his family could qualify for the Jewish "Righteous Among the Nations" award, given to non-Jewish people who have helped save lives during the Holocaust.

*An old Irish word for "very generous."

A photograph of the author's father, James Boylan,
taken on a business trip in Germany in the 1920s

Early baptism into Christianity

When I left primary school and began attending the local 'town school' run by the Christian Brothers, I was in for quite a shock. Not having received holy orders, members of this particular religious organisation are lay brothers rather than priests. Nonetheless, they are required to take vows of poverty and chastity and to dedicate their lives to the poor and to the education of the young, operating under a strict Catholic ethos. However, I discovered (unfortunately through experience) that their behaviour towards the pupils was far from Christian. The Brothers used to beat us with thick leather straps, purposely designed to deliver maximum pain and their control of the pupils by fear was even more frightening. I remember this really shocking me at the time as I expected that, at the very least, these teachers would have Christian values. However, looking back as an adult, I think that they were simply lost souls trying to cope with their lives.

Thankfully, there were a few very good lay teachers in the school who got us through the next five years of secondary education. But when I left in 1967, I was eighteen years of age with no idea of what I wanted to do with the rest of my life.

Like many others, I decided to head to London to work in a pub for the summer months. Although this gave me a little more experience of the world, I didn't see it as a long term option and returned to Ireland to seek work. I ended up in a temporary job in Dublin as a door-to-door salesman, which was certainly a different experience to a bartender. The job involved selling bibles, but not just any bible; I had to persuade people to purchase a huge, family bible that, at that time, cost the average weekly wage. It was a lavish publication with full-colour illustrations of the Vatican, its popes and all the saints. The company that sold the bibles was owned by an English Jew. It wasn't an easy job, as it was commission-based rather than salaried, so we had to "sell or leave" depending on our performance. The majority of my colleagues did the latter. I found dealing with insults particularly challenging and had to learn to ignore these and proceed to the next door with renewed optimism. However, I came into contact with a sufficient number of nice people to keep me feeling positive about the work. I also learned a lot about people and their individual outlook on life, and how this influenced the way they lived their lives on a day-to-day basis.

I think the following much-quoted statement from Dr. Wayne Dyer, American philosopher, self-help author and motivational speaker, sums this up well:

> "When you change the way you look at things, the things you look at change."

(Incidentally, Dyer's first book, *Your Erroneous Zones* (1976), is one of the best-selling books of all time, with an estimated 35 million copies sold to date.)

I remember knocking on doors in a new housing development in Dublin. Judging by appearances, the residents must have had hefty mortgages, so I didn't fancy my chances of selling many bibles. Indeed, the residents must have been used to door-to-door salesmen, because when I called at one particular house, the owner told me outright that he had no interest in buying. In fact, he said that, because of the high number of callers he received weekly, he'd just written a notice that he intended to put up on his door that very day. He showed me what he had composed and the first line of the notice said, "If you're selling something, I don't want it, and even if I do want it, I can't afford to buy it." As I looked at the words, a thought occurred to me and I grew quite excited.

"Hey, I could sell these!"

The man looked at me, obviously confused. I explained, "You see, this is something they do need in this estate. If you print up hundreds of them, I could sell them door to door."

Two days later, there was a letter to the editor of one of the national newspapers in Ireland with the heading, "Super Salesman." The man had provided a detailed description of me and related the whole story as an example of foresight and creativity.

Unfortunately, the manager of the company did not see it that way and called me to his office, where he gave me a telling off for generating "unfavourable publicity." Fortunately, I survived this experience and remained in the position!

My job continued to open my eyes to life in Ireland and, for the first time, I witnessed extremes of poverty. As I knocked on doors in various parts of the country, I found that life in cities such as Limerick was a real eye-opener. This was the setting of Frank McCourt's bestselling novel, *Angela's Ashes*, in which he described the impoverished circumstances of the people of Limerick and the extent of control that the Catholic Church had over them.

As I continued selling on doorsteps, I discovered that I related to people naturally, and could persuade them to buy, regardless of their financial situation. I began to do well and, even though I was only twenty at this stage, promotion to the position of supervisor with a company car followed. My role was to drive around Ireland with young recruits, training them in the art of selling. I really enjoyed this work and remained in the post for almost three years but once I'd saved enough money to set up a business I left. So by the age of twenty-one I had bought all the necessary equipment, my own car and had started working as a professional photographer with a fully equipped studio.

Early professional life

I didn't know it back then, of course, but professional photography would come to represent a very significant part of my working life (forty years) What I also realise now is that it was during my days as a photographer that I began to experience a certain freedom; a freedom of thought and from analytical reasoning which allowed my imagination and creative self to take over. This was when my results were most artistic.

Over many years, in order to be the best photographer I could be, I self-trained in the art of good photography practice as well as studying under various master photographers from America and the UK. It was during one such seminar that I discovered one of my most important lessons—if you always be your authentic self, your true brilliance will always come out.

Up until then, I had listened to the advice of a lot of different master photographers who offered many different ideas and techniques, all of which was very interesting and useful. However, there is a danger that we end up simply gathering ideas and copying the practice of others, rather than creating and expanding our own technique. Examining the work of master photographers is always going to be excellent for learning and this did provide me with confidence to achieve a certain level of results, but I did not consider the outcome to be totally my own. I needed to find a way to encourage my own creativity and talent to emerge, just as we all need to strive to develop our best potential in this life, be it in our work, our private life, our community or our spirituality.

It was during a training session with a UK photographer I greatly admired that I experienced such affirmation regarding my work. Despite studying and practicing photography intensely, I still suffered a lot of self-doubt and worried that I was merely copying the work of others, so I had asked him to provide me with an honest appraisal of my work. At his request I supplied a sample of fifty photographs that I'd recently taken and waited nervously for his response. However, I was elated when he said that it was evident in the photographs that I had a distinctive style, and advised me to continue doing "my own thing."

Naturally this increased my confidence, and taught me to trust my insight, not to overthink things, and not to mimic what others were doing.

This encouragement changed my life as a photographer as I was able to trust myself enough to capture the photograph I'd envisioned, even before taking it. The same process is helping me change as a spiritual person and as a healer.

Time to be me

I have read all the books, now it is time to be me.

We must learn to trust this statement as it is relevant for all of us, in *every* part of our lives – our relationships, our jobs, our leisure time, and when we have to make decisions, whether they be small or the most important life choices we will make: if we do this from our authentic self, it will be correct for us.

So how do we do this? Well first of all, we need a moment to turn off the 60,000 thoughts that invade our mind every day and learn how to empty it. But what remains is not "nothing"; we are simply making space to allow the Divine, or knowledge of the universe, to be with us.

A close up of a butterfly by the author

Wedding days

So, thanks to my newfound confidence, I continued to enjoy working as a photographer and found that my skills were in demand within my local community and beyond. I felt privileged when asked to cover weddings and private celebrations for families, as this involved becoming intimate with their lives for a short time. As part of their "big day," clients often confided in me or asked for my professional advice regarding the event, particularly during major functions; I must say, I enjoyed this intimacy and shared many joyful moments and insightful experiences with my clients. I undertook a lot of work in this area of photography along the border area of Ireland, both north and south (as I mentioned at the beginning of this chapter, Northern Ireland is part of the United Kingdom and Southern Ireland is a Republic.) At the time, during the 1970s and 80s, there was a war situation in Ireland. I go into this in more detail later in this book but, briefly, the IRA (Irish Republican Army) whose primary goal was to force the UK to negotiate a withdrawal from Northern Ireland, was carrying out a bombing campaign and killing members of the British Army in Northern Ireland.

I remember covering a wedding during the height of "The Troubles", and it turned out the groom was a leading member of the IRA and was on the run from the security forces in Northern Ireland. When the church ceremony had ended, and just before departure to the hotel for the reception, which was across the border in Southern Ireland, I was told that I wasn't required to go to the hotel. As the wedding photographer, I found this very upsetting, as I had always provided a very professional service, resulting the best photographic record of the big day as possible. I had planned my best work would be in the beautiful gardens of the hotel. I insisted, despite the order to the contrary, on following through with my plans and drove to the hotel. Upon arrival, I understood why I had been instructed not to attend; the IRA had taken over the hotel and there were men with machine guns positioned on the roof. Nevertheless,

I was already there, so I set to work anyway and completed the job, and the newlyweds were very pleased.

On another occasion, my assignment was to cover the wedding of the daughter of an English lord. The man owned a large estate in Southern Ireland and the reception was to be held in his stately home. Until the day of the wedding, I was unaware that the groom was a British Army officer and that many of the guests were high-ranking officers who had travelled from England for the reception. At this point in time, British Army officers were prime targets by the IRA in Ireland so, not surprisingly, the security at the wedding was intense. I recall men in plain clothes arriving at the church. They began to assemble large machine guns and left the building to take up positions on the roof.

This particular job was definitely not what you would call "run of the mill," but as I was employed for my creative skills I had to deliver the goods, despite the tension of the situation. I must admit though, I did have problems keeping the security officers and their rifles out of the background in the wedding photographs!

I also recall covering the wedding of a captain in the Special Security Forces in Northern Ireland. He was marrying a girl from my town in Southern Ireland and I will call him "George" for the sake of confidentiality. Officers from Northern Ireland were not allowed travel into Southern Ireland as this put them in great danger of being killed. However, George's wedding was in Southern Ireland, he had obviously had special permission to be married in the Republic. As we travelled from the church to the reception, the bride and groom's car was accompanied by a police escort, so yet again I found myself surrounded by security services as I worked. The couple lived in Northern Ireland and I was saddened to learn that his wife died tragically some years later.

About two years after this, I attended a wedding of a couple in a church in Northern Ireland, whose reception was being held in the South. I was surprised to see George at the wedding, and was shocked to see him travel with all the other guests across the border to the location of the reception. I knew he was in great danger of being an IRA target. I decided to approach the plain clothes policemen (Gardai) during the reception and explained my fears for this man. They agreed that he was in great danger and would do their best to protect him. Later they contacted me and revealed that they had kept him under supervision all day and even escorted him as far as the border that evening, without him knowing anything about it. I have many other stories of similar events during my working life.

During my long photographic career I was not particularly spiritual, although, looking back, I realise that I was actually "switched on" to my higher self and inspiration was flowing back then; I must have instinctively relied on this when I was required to be creative. Some such moments from this period of my life are really vivid and remain with me to this day.

I recall when I decided to photograph some of the well-known, elderly characters in my town and hold an exhibition of the final portraits for a local charity. For me, this really was a labour of love, and I photographed each of them mostly in their own environment, in order to capture their "real selves".

I entitled the exhibition "Memory of My Father", inspired by a poem of the same name written by a famous Irish poet from my county, Patrick Kavanagh.

Memory of My Father

Every old man I see
Reminds me of my father
When he had fallen in love with death
One time when sheaves were gathered.

That man I saw in Gardiner Street
Stumble on the kerb was one,
He stared at me half-eyed,
I might have been his son.

And I remember the musician
Faltering over his fiddle
In Bayswater, London.
He too set me the riddle.

Every old man I see
In October-coloured weather
Seems to say to me
"I was once your father."

Patrick Kavanagh, 1904-1967

I recall with fondness a man called Tommy, who was one of my "subjects" for the exhibition. His passion was playing the violin, old Irish tunes in particular, so I suggested that I photograph him playing in the studio. A friend had accompanied him and when he began to play for him, I could see that Tommy had completely forgotten that I was taking his portrait. He was so completely absorbed in the beautiful Irish air he was playing that I am convinced he no longer knew I was in the room. I, too, became completely absorbed and was determined to properly capture this moment, in order to reflect the intense emotion that his playing evoked. So I turned down the studio lighting, using only faint back light on Tommy and the strings on his bow. It was a truly memorable experience, proving that when you work and view life from the heart, beautiful moments occur.

For another project, I was commissioned to photograph some important, very old Irish archaeology sites. I really got absorbed in this assignment as I could feel the importance of these sites and the old stone forts that were still standing on them. I spent days absorbing their history and photographed them to reflect their mystical presence, very often at dawn or sunset, but also during the day for more dramatic effects with silhouettes and backlighting.

I recall one moment in my studio after photographing a twelve-year-old girl. I always used beautiful, gentle music to create atmosphere, in order to relax the sitters and open myself to inspiration. This worked so well during this particular sitting that the girl, her parents and I were all practically in a trance. When the little girl was leaving, she turned at the door, looked back into the studio and said, "Goodbye, magical place." I have never forgotten her words.

Fairy Fort near the author's house

CHAPTER 2

FINDING THE PATH

I was in class on a normal school day in Ireland when the teacher asked me the name of the capital of Bulgaria. To the surprise of all in the room – and myself more than anyone – I instinctively provided the correct answer, despite never having studied anything about the country previous to this. However, I definitely seemed to have had some sort of "link" to Bulgaria and it was to have a great influence on me in later years.

My first visit to the country was unplanned. In 1980 my wife and I were asked if we'd like to complete the numbers on an excursion as two extra adults on a school skiing trip to the Southern Bulgarian mountains, close to the Greek border. At that time, Bulgaria was still a communist country, situated behind the "Iron Curtain", as it became popularly known after former British prime minister Winston Churchill referred to it many years ago.

After just a few days, I instinctively knew that Bulgaria was my spiritual home, and I quickly felt a real closeness to the people, their language and their customs. I remember thinking how strange it felt to be in a strictly communist country for the first time. Outside the resort, people looked at us with a degree of suspicion, as they had undoubtedly been taught by the system that we "Westerners" were different, and that we'd come from a suspect regime that was plotting the overthrow of their way of life. This was compounded when we ventured into the local town by taxi, as opposed to participating on guided tours. The townspeople did stop to stare at us, but somehow I knew that despite their caution and apprehension, they were genuine, decent people. Indeed, beyond their guarded exterior, I was delighted to discover a warm, and indeed extremely spiritual, people.

We were visiting, at that time, a communist country whose people had no incentive to work, but were well-trained in tourism services. Once, on our way by taxi to the town, we became stuck for a while on the mountain road due to a snowstorm, and I had opportunity to communicate with the taxi driver. I noticed that he had a picture of Stalin on display in his car and I commented on this. He became very animated and held up his fist in a victory sign, extolling the greatness of Joseph Stalin, former leader of the Soviet Union.

Along with the special partnership enjoyed with my wife, my long association with Bulgaria would prove to be of enormous help in developing the spiritual side of myself during my life, both when I was developing my photography business and later, my overseas real estate business. That first visit was so important, as it was the beginning of my very long association and spiritual journey with Bulgaria.

The Great Escape

In the late eighties, I was given a book by an old friend that set me on my path of spiritual discovery. It was titled, *In the Light of Truth—A Grail Message*. I did not agree with everything contained in the book, but it certainly opened my mind to new possibilities. It also changed the way I thought about God and the universe and helped me to move on from a very set position, which was one that I'd never really come to accept from either a strict Catholic, or indeed Protestant, religion.

At this time, we were travelling to Bulgaria on our annual skiing holiday while the country was still under the rule of communism. Many of the ski instructors and the staff in the hotels in the resort where we stayed were anti-communist and felt that their freedom was being restricted. They thought that the government's control over them was greatly inhibiting their lives; in other words, they were not free to decide for themselves where they could live and work in their own country. In addition, because of the influx of visitors to the country, they could see the affluence of us Westerners (relatively speaking) and how we had the freedom to work for ourselves. We began to take over Western clothes and music for our Bulgarian friends, as well as books for those who had a real passion for reading literature that was not available behind the Iron Curtain. One of these was Jimmy, a very rebellious ski instructor, who often said, "Bring me over books I cannot get in this country." So I took him over the book *In the Light of Truth*. Of course, spiritual books were banned by the authorities, as religion was frowned upon, and the attitude was that any such spirituality was simply for suspicious old people. In fact, we came to learn that undercover agents watched who attended church on Sundays in the local villages. If any of the ski instructors or other staff at the resort went to a service, they would no doubt have lost their jobs and been moved away to another part of the Country, out of contact with any tourists.

I must admit, I honestly thought that Jimmy would not understand the complex message contained in the book. However, he relished it and said that as a result of reading it, he felt an even greater desire for freedom – not only his physical freedom, but also spiritual freedom.

One day, he called me aside on the ski slope and said, "Come, let's ski on the black run." Now for those who aren't aware, this is the most difficult slope, but it was obvious that Jimmy did not want the secret security police to see us chatting, or overhear our conversation.

When we got there, he said,

"Sean, the book you gave me spoke about us having a free spirit. It says we are more than just this body. I cannot stay in this fucking country any longer, completely restricted in my being. I'm going to escape from Bulgaria to the West."

I replied, "Jim, you cannot do this. It's impossible. You'll be caught."

"I am not staying here. Someday, I will be free."

And that was that. We skied down the piste and I went on with my holiday, returning home as normal.

About four months later, my phone rang.

"Sean, this is Jimmy from Bulgaria. I escaped. I am in Belfast."

I couldn't believe my ears! I immediately invited him to our home and he arrived the very next day, and we sat up late into the evening as Jimmy recounted the amazing account of his escape. It turned out that he had been imprisoned for his liberal views on freedom and anti-communist activities. However, he said that while in jail, he'd become friendly with the prison governor and that once this man learned that, as well as being an excellent ski instructor, Jimmy was an all-around sportsman, he asked him to give tennis lessons to his wife. The governor's house was close to the Bulgarian/Greek border and since Greece was a western Country, Jimmy found himself close to the border between Eastern and Western Europe. So, not long after arriving at the governor's house to give his wife tennis lessons, Jimmy ran for the hills and the forest. This turned out to be his path to freedom.

However, the path wasn't an easy one, as the area consisted of many, many kilometres of scrub and thick brush, and Jimmy said that he had to run until almost at the state of collapse. But he had to keep going, travelling mostly at night, as most of those who lived in the area at that time would have been spies. He said that if he'd been seen, those people would undoubtedly have informed on him.

When he finally arrived at the high, border fence, his relief was short lived when an alert sounded, and all hell broke loose. It turned out that an East German couple who had been trying to cross at the same time had attracted the attention of the border guards. So Jimmy had to retreat and lie low. He slept in the forest during the day and returned the following night. This time he came prepared with some old car tyres. He tied these together and threw them over the fence, which meant he could climb over without being electrocuted.

It's hard to describe the elation I felt as Jimmy described his excitement at seeing an old Volkswagen Beetle on a small road. Because this car wasn't available in Bulgaria at that time, he knew that he'd reached the West … and was finally free.

Jimmy's strength and athleticism of course played a huge role during his escape across the Iron Curtain. However, I came to learn that what was equally important was his belief in his own spiritual ability to overcome such a seemingly impossible challenge.

This is a lesson for us all. Jimmy was branded a criminal by the authorities in Bulgaria because he wanted to be free. Many years later, his story would serve as inspiration to me when I was faced with a difficult situation here in Ireland. I too was accused of being a criminal. Faced with such challenges, it is so important that we remember why we chose a certain path and reassure ourselves that we did it for the right reason. Deep inside, if we hold onto our respect for ourselves and for others, we can be certain that we did not intend to offend and must continue to believe in our own integrity. This is what is most important and we too can manifest our dreams when we have sufficient conviction and faith in ourselves.

CHAPTER 3

COMMUNICATIONS

An introduction to Hay House Radio and further developments

*Early morning mysticism – photograph taken
by the author at Cootehill, Ireland*

Something strange happened as I was driving to Dublin one morning, resulting in what was to be a significant life change for me. I had been listening to a radio programme in the car for a while when, for no reason, it suddenly changed to an American radio station. This was a complete surprise to me as I had no access to the internet so couldn't stream international radio. Anyway, the feature was about spirituality so naturally I was interested, and when the interviewer mentioned another station,

"Hay House Radio," I felt compelled to write this name down. As soon as I came to a halt at the traffic lights I did this — just in time, since the programme disappeared and I was once again listening to Irish radio, with the same broadcaster talking about the country's problems.

I firmly believe that I was meant to hear about this American radio station that particular day, because of the strange way in which I learned about it. That evening I researched Hay House on my iPhone and discovered that the organization, which is primarily a publisher, has a mission to promote self-help and personal growth through inspirational and transformational books and products conducive to healing the planet. I must admit, my contact with Hay House has contributed vastly to my spiritual progress, introduced a whole new way of thinking for me, and continues to inspire though spiritual books.

In one of the books, I began to read about chakras, which are various focal points in the subtle, or non-physical, body. They are used in a variety of meditation practices for physical, emotional, mental and spiritual health. One section of the book particularly resonated with me, as it instructed the reader to keep their heart open and to say every day, "I open my heart to hope, harmony, laughter and love." In fact, this more or less became a daily mantra for me, as it encouraged a new openness in thought and purpose. I became aware of a growing ability to control my thoughts and realised that I could influence my positivity through this practice.

Further psychic experiences

*Photograph of a butterfly common to the Irish
landscape that is home for the author*

At 2:00 am on April 1, 2015, I experienced a strange phenomenon. I was awakened abruptly when my body began to vibrate and I felt a strong tingling sensation running from my head down to my feet. Although it startled me, it wasn't entirely unpleasant and I remember having the distinct impression that I was receiving some sort of energy. I wanted to let my wife know, so that she too could experience it, so I called for her to place her arms around me. However, no sound emerged. Suddenly, I became aware of lights above me and could make out a figure. This was someone I didn't recognize but, because of the goodness it radiated, I knew this was a beautiful spirit. I felt very disappointed when it disappeared as quickly as it arrived.

Two nights later, at precisely the same time, I felt a light sensation pass through my body. This time, to my amazement, my bed appeared to shift and move from the bedroom to the hallway – with me in it! It was at this point that I felt the presence of my deceased father, who had passed away when I was fourteen. He was with me, guiding the bed, and I felt totally safe. I thanked the heavens for what was happening and said, "I will travel with love." In fact, I remember smiling about this and saying to myself that the whole experience was as if I were on a bus journey, and my bed was the bus. The "bus" then reversed and returned to its usual place in the room. I said to my father, "So this is the Glaslough bus!" I was referring to a humorous story he and I had shared about an old neighbour Billy. You see, Glaslough was the name of the village close to where I was born, and the location of my family home. For years, Billy had claimed the "Blind Pension," despite being able to see. He had finally been caught out in the cinema in Monaghan, the nearest town, by the inspector responsible for assessing and allocating claims. The story goes that when Billy spotted the inspector, he shouted in the cinema at the top of his voice, "Am I on the Glaslough bus?" I shared the story once again with my spirit guide that morning, my father.

When I told a local psychic of this remarkable event, she explained to me that this was known as "astral travel." Astral travel or projection is an out-of-body experience in which the consciousness, spirit or subtle body separates from the physical body to travel outside it throughout the universe.

A photograph of the city of Istanbul taken by the author

My "ordination"

I have had many spiritual experiences over the last few years. In 2014, I was on an early morning flight to Sofia, via Brussels. As we flew over Europe, I had a very profound, spiritual experience. This time, I was awake and the event lasted for almost half an hour, during which I had the profoundly lucid impression that I had had been "ordained to heal." I find it very difficult to express exactly what took place in words, but I know that it was real. Before this, I had been told by several psychics that I possessed healing abilities, or rather that Jesus would heal people through me. I felt on that plane flying over Europe, that my gift of healing had just been magnified.

When I arrived at Sofia, I joked to myself about what had just happened on the flight. This is something I have always been able to do after a spiritual experience. Anyway, at that stage I'd been a professional photographer for well over thirty years, and had undertaken many assignments capturing celebrations in the life of family groups and couples. And, just as the wedding day is one of the most important for a young couple, the ordination ceremony performed by a bishop is considered the most important day in a priest's life. On landing in Sofia following the revelation and confirmation of my healing abilities, this suddenly came to mind and I smiled to myself, joking that I had somehow just been "ordained." Indeed, my imagination went into overdrive and I pictured myself receiving photographs of my own "big day!"

CHAPTER 4

AURAS AND LIGHT

Sunset on Ireland's western coast photographed by the author

About this time, I began to see what appeared to be auras and flashing lights around the people I met. This began in Bulgaria, during one of my many visits to Sofia. I was in church one Sunday morning when, during the service, I suddenly noticed a trace of white light surrounding each member of the congregation. When I looked at the altar, I could see that the priest had a similar aura, exactly like a halo.

After leaving the service, I went to a local café and sat by the window so that I could look out at the street. As I relaxed over my coffee and gazed out, I began to notice something. It was almost as though what had happened in church had been some sort of "training" for my psychic muscles, as if in preparation for another level of spiritual development. Yet again, I find it difficult to describe the phenomenon in words, but when I concentrated on pedestrians as they passed the café window or crossed the street, I could suddenly see what looked like a double image of each person. Everyone appeared to have a second image of themselves at a slight distance from their physical body and every movement they made was replicated, so that when they walked, I could see two sets of their arms and legs moving in unison. It was almost as if I was seeing their spirit or astral body, but I have yet to receive an exact explanation of what this was. I began seeing this on a regular basis but back then I had only experienced this phenomenon in Bulgaria. In more recent times it has happened in Ireland, but on a much less regular basis. Whenever I witnessed these auras around people, it was never frightening or strange; in fact, I felt privileged and happy to be permitted to witness what might have been their spirits.

It may be a complete coincidence, but even more recently after starting to study a course in fairyology, I began to see tiny, flashing lights at the sides of my eyes. This has been explained by some spiritualists as seeing spirits or angels. I'm still not sure which they were, but these moving lights still happen daily and I am grateful for the experience.

A while ago I received an offer to have my eyes tested for reading glasses and made an appointment. When the optician asked me how my eyes were working, I decided not to mention my "visions" as he would probably have misunderstood!

A white butterfly photographed by the author near his home in Ireland

A family tragedy

My spiritual awareness underwent a significant development, regrettably as a result of tragedy in our lives. Many years earlier, my older brother had taken over the family business manufacturing concrete products. He'd made a great success of it, but in 1991 he had been going through a very difficult time, which ended in his sudden disappearance. We discovered afterwards that he had taken a boat to Scotland, where he had ended his life by disappearing into the sea and his body was never found.

My last meeting with him before this event was very unfortunate. He had been a guest at a wedding at which I was the photographer, and he'd reprimanded me for taking too long and causing delays to proceedings. I understood that he had not being feeling well and that it wasn't his fault, but I was saddened that we had parted on such terms. After the shock surrounding his death and, while the authorities were searching for his body, I experienced a huge shift in my life priorities and indeed became much more aware of the afterlife. In fact, I went to a medium, which was quite unusual after such an event at that time in Ireland. To my astonishment, my brother made contact and apologised to me for being rude the last time we'd spoken. Of course, there was no need for such an apology as I'd long since forgiven him, but happily we have now become very close in spirit.

In the late nineties, I began to receive clear messages that I should change my life and career. This really surprised me, as I had always enjoyed working in photography. However, I eventually decided to follow this advice and sold my business to a trainee photographer, who had been a student of mine up until then.

This newfound freedom provided me with several opportunities but, because of my knowledge of Bulgaria and closeness to its people, it seemed like a natural progression to draw upon my experience of that country in order to help Irish people seeking to purchase a property there. So I decided to set up in business providing advice to clients interested in property investment in Bulgaria.

CHAPTER 5

MAJOR CHANGES

A chance encounter with a brave little girl

I continued to make annual trips to Bulgaria during the eighties and nineties and, in 1992, was introduced to a remarkable Bulgarian child. Our meeting came about after a ski instructor told us of the plight of a local family whose young daughter was in a life-or-death situation. He explained that the little girl, Theodora, had a very rare condition and as a result had to follow a special diet. Her parents had tried everything to acquire a supply of the particular food that she urgently required, but it was prohibitively expensive. He added that she would probably have to take this special food for the rest of her life, therefore a regular supply would be needed to save her. It was such a devastating story, we decided to visit the family the next evening.

The ski instructor went along with us to act as interpreter, and introduced us to the three-and-a-half-year-old Theodora and her family. Her parents told me that their daughter had been diagnosed with Phenylketonuria or PKU, a rare but potentially serious, inherited disorder. When I researched this condition later, I discovered that a person with PKU is unable to break down the amino acid phenylalanine. It builds up in the blood and brain, potentially leading to brain damage.

It turned out that Theodora had been assigned to a doctor in Sofia, a specialist in the condition, who had told them that she would have to be fed a special protein diet formula with reduced phenylalanine. He said that, with monitoring, she should be fine provided that she follow this strict diet for the rest of her life. However, her parents explained that the annual cost of the diet formula was out of their reach. They had tried everything to get it, and Theodora's father told me that he had even gone to the Bulgarian Minister of Health and got down on his knees to plead for help, but they still were not provided with supplies.

Her mother showed me a small tin of the formula – the last remaining from those that had been donated by an Austrian tourist. It was a cheaper version of what Theodora required and was very unpalatable for a child because it tasted so strong, but it was all they had at that point. I took photograph of Theodora along with the tin of the food, which I still have to this day.

After this, Theodora's mother suddenly looked directly into my eyes and said something in Bulgarian; I will never forget the moment. Our ski instructor translated what she had just said.

"We have had lots of promises by tourists who come here to ski, but nothing has happened. We have only this small amount of powder left in this tin. Are you going to save my daughter?"

The ski instructor said, "She just needs to know now."

I thought about this for one moment, nodded and said, "Yes."

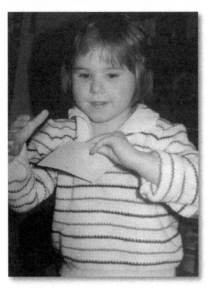

*Photograph taken by the author of Theodora
on the day he was introduced to her mother*

When we were going down the steps from their house, my friend turned to me and asked how exactly we were going to do this, since we didn't have the money. I replied that we would just have to try, but my mind was already formulating a plan.

You see, at that time, I was a member of the Rotary Club in Monaghan, where I had been assigned to the setting up of a "Rotaract" Club for the under eighteen-year-olds of the town. This was a junior version of our Rotary Club, a group of local people dedicated to helping their community and to fostering cooperation with other clubs across Ireland. The Rotaract Club was well established by then and I felt that there was real potential for achieving great things. It was this I had in mind as I descended the steps of Theodora's family home. I truly believed that this project would be a suitable challenge for the club and provide the members with great experience.

On my return to Ireland, I immediately made contact with a specialist dietician in a Dublin hospital and explained about the little girl's predicament. She kindly provided samples of the special diet food and said that I should send it to Bulgaria for Theodora to test under the supervision of her parents and doctors. Within a week we had sent the samples and a reply from Bulgaria that it was perfect for her. All we needed to do next was to raise the money to buy the first year's supply – this would be the challenge.

When I met with our Rotaract Club, I was very enthusiastic about us being able to help Theodora and her family and was still convinced that it would be a prefect project for the members. What I ought to have been less forthcoming about was that the special diet would, most probably, need to be supplied for life.

In fact, this announcement caused much concern among the members. They felt nervous about such a great responsibility and said that such a commitment was much too great for them to undertake. The club declared that the project simply could not be taken on. Naturally, I was devastated.

However, an old friend of mine, Peter O'Reilly (now deceased) could see my extreme disappointment. He said to me, "Sean, we will do this." He was such a great soul and he lobbied our Rotary Club and got others clubs involved to help. Eventually we had sufficient support to begin fundraising and the Monaghan Rotary Club agreed to manage the project.

The big push to raise funds began and little Theodora's parents were naturally overjoyed when they learned that their daughter was to be given this lifeline. Bulgaria had just left the Communist Regime and there were no public funds for such a diet, so fundraising continued and the food was sent for about twenty years until, finally, the Bulgarian government was in a position to supply most of Theodora's requirements.

Theodora is now thirty-one years old and works in the local municipality office. Her name translates as "Child of God" and she really is. Everyone who has met Theodora loves her and she and her family have brought great blessings to us all and great love to me in particular. In fact, they are like members of our extended family for my relatives and friends in Monaghan.

The Irish people were very supportive of this project, and especially those in my own community. As you can imagine, a lot of fundraising was required to send funds for the cost of the special food every year that we took with us on our annual ski trip to the mountains on the Greek border. This delivery was of great joy for all of us involved and usually Theodora's father would cook a mountain lamb or other such feast for us. There was such an exchange of love that I had never experienced before.

I have been asked in the past why the Irish give so generously to all charitable pleas, particularly for food and shelter; I believe that the answer lies in the Great Famine in Ireland from 1845 to 1847, during which over one million people died of hunger because of the failure of the potato crop. Another million people perished on the "famine ships" that left these shores to go to America, in an attempt to escape the situation. The facts about this disaster are studied in history lessons throughout schools in Ireland and it definitely remains in the Irish psyche; so I believe it is for this reason that, if they have the means to help the needy, the people of Ireland tend to respond with as much generosity as they can afford.

When Theodora was seventeen, I was extremely honoured when her family invited me to a very special occasion – her graduation from high school. This is a very important day for Bulgarians as the whole village celebrates, and the new graduates parade through the town with their family and friends. I will never forgot that day and was very emotional as I was driven with Theodora's parents, grandparents, uncles and aunts through the town.

Photo of Theodora taken by the author on the day of her graduation

Considering the amount of fundraising that had been carried out in the community over the years for Theodora, we thought it would be a nice idea to invite her to Ireland so she could meet the people who had been helping her. So it was another wonderful day when she came to Monaghan and thanked the locals for their gift of life and to assure everyone that she was now in good health and looking forward to the rest of her life. The public address she gave in front of the then President of Ireland, Mary Robinson, specially invited visitors from UK and US Rotary Clubs, and almost a thousand delegates from the whole island of Ireland was extremely emotional.

The fact that Theodora was able to stand in front of us all and give such a speech was an incredibly moving moment, considering that without that special diet, she may not have been alive or, at the very least, would have had severe physical and learning difficulties. Everyone listening felt so privileged and fortunate to be able to share that moment when a young Bulgarian woman thanked the Irish people for her life.

Difficult days

Over the years, Theodora's parents told us many stories about life in their mountain village and in their country. At the beginning of the Communist Regime and end of World War II, they explained that her great-grandfather on her father's side was murdered by communists. He had been in business at the time and, when they took over leadership of the country, they killed him and took over his shop and business because he refused to join the Communist Party.

During one of our visits we went to the village of Samakov, where Theodora's grandparents lived close to the large ski resort of Borovits. While we were there, her grandfather recounted the story of one evening when the Communist Party held a party night in Borovits, in a lodge formerly owned by the deposed tsar of Bulgaria. The grandfather, son of the murdered man, was a very accomplished accordion player and excellent singer and the party sent for him and requested that he entertain them. He told me that it was the most difficult thing he had ever had to do in his life – to play and sing for the very people who had murdered his father as they partied and enjoyed themselves.

Theodora's father also told me that he had once been advised by the leader of the party at the time that if he wanted to progress in his career as a veterinarian, he must join the Communist Party. He pleaded with the man not to force him to join, as it would be too painful, considering that his grandfather had been murdered by communists in previous years. He suggested that, as a compromise, he would join the Agrarian Party which organised farmers and other rural workers, and was the only other party permitted to exist in Bulgaria at the time. He said that he had been more than relieved when allowed to do so.

A visit to a Bulgarian orphanage

Not long after the fall of communism in Bulgaria, we learned that orphanages there were experiencing major difficulties. Theodora's father and a ski instructor friend named Bojo, who were great humanitarians, decided to do some research in order to find out what was needed. They informed us that blankets, clothes and medicines were desperately required. Once back in Ireland, we set about collecting all these items and took a consignment back to Bulgaria with us. We hired a jeep and filled it full of supplies and headed off to the mountains to deliver the goods. Unfortunately the snow was extremely deep and we became stuck, causing us to be delayed. However, after digging ourselves out we eventually arrived at the remote orphanage at the end of a road, deep in the mountains.

The director was very courteous and it was obvious that she was trying to do everything she could for the orphanage, but said that there was no money available for anything. In fact, the value of the Bulgarian lev had fallen a hundredfold, and the country was experiencing hyperinflation with resulting soaring prices and shortages of everything. She then gave us a tour of the orphanage and we were totally unprepared for what we were about to see.

The building consisted of many rooms that were filled with high-sided beds, each occupied by a child. It seemed that many of these little ones had not left their bed in years because of the deformity of their limbs. Admittedly, this may have been due to a childhood condition rather than lack of movement, but their legs and hands had grown inwards. It truly was a terrible scene, like something from the Dark Ages, and the smell was overwhelming. I attempted to take some photographs, in order to record the desperate situation, but found it extremely difficult. None of us were able to speak, as we were so shocked by the plight of these children. The fact that they could still give us a smile and hold out their hands to greet us was heart-breaking. Despite the language barrier and their obvious discomfort, they gave us a warm greeting and seemed so grateful for their new blankets. To be honest, we were all moved to tears.

After the tour, the director invited us to her office and asked us what we thought of everything we had just seen. We were so shocked, we were unable to speak for some time.

As we were leaving, a young girl approached us and handed me a present. It was a small dog, which I was told she had knitted. It meant more to me than I am able to describe, and I still have that little dog to this day.

We returned to Ireland and arranged to have more supplies and help delivered on a regular basis. Eventually, other orphanages began to receive assistance and some were voluntarily painted by some of the ski instructors from the resorts. My friend told me they had been encouraged to take action after learning of all the support and donations from the Irish.

Picture of present given to the author in the orphanage.

CHAPTER 6

TROUBLE CLOSE TO HOME

In the early 1970's, the political conflict known as "The Troubles," had grown increasingly serious in Ireland. Activity had heightened, with bombings and killings on an almost daily basis and although this was mostly in Northern Ireland, the violence sometimes spilled over into parts of the Republic of Ireland, England and occasionally mainland Europe.

May 17, 1974 was the date of the highest death toll in any single day during The Troubles in Ireland. That Friday afternoon, during rush hour, a series of three co-ordinated bombs, planted by Loyalist paramilitaries, were set off in the centre of Dublin, killing twenty-seven and injuring hundreds. Shortly afterwards, a fourth bomb went off in the centre of my home town of Monaghan, five kilometres (about three miles) from the border with Northern Ireland. The explosion was outside a lounge bar, killing seven people and injuring many more, both young and old.

On that particular day, I had been delivering photographs to a local priest and had just left him to drive back into town when the bomb was detonated. Although I was four kilometres (two and a half miles) from the scene of the explosion, I felt the impact but had no idea what it was. In fact, I stopped my car and checked to see if there was a fault with the engine and, when I failed to find anything, continued on my journey. As I drove through the outskirts of town, I soon became aware that there had been a huge explosion. I remember thinking how dark everything appeared; there was a black cloud, literally and metaphorically, over the town, and total mayhem at the scene. Police officers were shouting orders to follow the perpetrators, sirens of arriving ambulances were blaring, and flames were coming from a nearby café. There was a sense of shock, panic and confusion and then I saw those who had been injured and killed. I remember having a debate with myself about photographing the scene; I didn't want to, as it felt like I would have been intruding, or somehow exploiting the situation. But then I made a decision—the world needed to witness this atrocity, to see the devastating results of a bomb in a town centre. My studio wasn't far, so I ran and got my camera and started photographing the scene. Shortly afterwards, news editors from the national newspapers began to call me to request the photographs. This was at the time when film had to be processed and printed but, fortunately, I was able to do this immediately in my darkroom. I then drove to Dublin with the results. Next morning, the shocking images of the atrocity were there for the whole world to see.

Twenty-five years later, the local municipality invited families of the deceased, firefighters, police officers and all those civilians who had helped on that tragic day to the unveiling of a memorial to mark the event. I was also invited and, at the commemorative luncheon afterwards, for the first time in twenty-five years I was able to talk about my experience of that day. It was very emotional, as those who had been caught up in the incident shared memories of what had happened in our small town of just 7,000 inhabitants all those years earlier.

Bridging the divide

The Rotary organization in Ireland was unusual as it was a single district incorporating both Northern Ireland and Southern Ireland.

The Rotary movement was formed in America at the beginning of the twentieth century with the ethos "Service above Self." Basically, it brings together business and professional people who volunteer their time and skills to help promote understanding in their community, and around the world. All the clubs in Ireland, north and south, belonged to a single district and they met weekly. Religion was not an issue, and there was mutual respect among members, regardless of their religious or political affiliations. This was unusual during such a period of serious political and religious divide; because they were from different cultures, club members would have been educated at a school for their particular religion, meaning that most would have had very few occasions to meet in the past.

As a truly international organisation that is open to all, regardless of race, colour, religion, gender, or political preference, I believed passionately that Rotary was in an excellent position to promote political and religious tolerance in communities across the island of Ireland, and to actively promote peace in our divided country.

Before my election to the role of president of our local club in 1988/89, I called a meeting with four of my fellow presidents in clubs from both Northern and Southern Ireland. We formed a committee under the acronym TABU—"Towards a Better Understanding" which aimed to bring Catholic and Protestant communities together, in order to help them recognize their similarities rather than differences. Although we had many supporters, we also had critics within Rotary who thought that we should not get involved in such an undertaking. However, I and the rest of the committee felt that history would judge us harshly if we did not use our influence to encourage our divided communities to come together for the betterment of all.

I addressed the general assembly at the all-Ireland Rotary meeting and throughout the year I visited all the clubs individually with the small committee that we had formed. I always began by quoting the following from Edmond Burke, Anglo-Irish statesman and philosopher:

> "The only thing necessary for evil to triumph is for good men to do nothing."

Pupils of different religions in Ireland for the most part are not educated together and attend either a Catholic or Protestant school. This can result in a lot of misunderstanding and mistrust of "the other side" due to ignorance of each other's cultures.

To start with, we produced a booklet on shared education called *Mutual Understanding*, which was later used as a model for education in Northern Ireland. We then invited a club in Chicago to host a group of six Protestant and six Catholic students from both Northern Ireland and Southern Ireland. They travelled to America together and each student qualified for the trip by submitting an essay on the topic of conflict resolution. The US trip resulted in new friendships across the divide and the exercise was repeated on an annual basis after this first, successful venture.

The Parliamentary Under Secretary of State for Northern Ireland at the time, Dr Brian Mawhinney, was a forward-thinking man. He agreed to meet our committee and gave us every encouragement to continue with our objective of creating greater links and, therefore understanding, between the communities. The framework for this committee's work was later used by the Department of Education in Northern Ireland in order to educate young people of different religions together. The Secretary of State wrote to us, saying, "This initiative by Rotary represents a major response to our call. I am sure it will be immensely successful and will establish a model for many others to follow."

If ever we needed reassurance of how small steps could achieve great results, this was it, truly demonstrating how we can all make a real difference to better our world.

Bringing parties together

The next step for our committee was to arrange meetings with peace workers from both sides of the divide in Belfast. All had been seeking solutions for bringing people together, but they were from opposing sides of the community. So we met with social workers in loyalist areas of Belfast (a loyalist refers to a hard-line, Protestant unionist, strongly favouring the political union between Great Britain and Northern Ireland.) and meetings also took place with social workers from republican areas of Belfast (generally speaking, a republican is a Catholic nationalist who wants to have a united Ireland, completely free from British rule.)

We managed to bring all parties together in a safe, neutral environment for a whole weekend. I found it extremely difficult to believe that these people were practically neighbours, undertaking social work for their local community in difficult areas, without ever having met each other. At that time, communities that existed side by side were completely divided, not only in their religion and political beliefs, but by physical walls that had been built through cities and towns where republicans and loyalists lived in close proximity. When the social workers began to talk to each other, they realised how much they had in common. It's true to say that amazing things happened that weekend. We had taken these people out of their communities to a retreat centre in County Fermanagh, a county famous for its lakes and scenery, which was conducive to relaxing and opening up to each other. During a special programme of workshops that weekend individuals talked openly and honestly, with the outcome that we, the organisers, as well as the delegates learned that there were no real divisions between people—only perceived differences. When the participants returned to their individual communities, we kept in contact with them and learned that they had kept in contact with each other. So lessons had been learned by all of us over that very emotional weekend.

I was encouraged to investigate other, practical ways to advance peace in Ireland in a practical way. Being a member of Rotary, and the fact that I was chairman of TABU, I believed that it was my duty to attempt this, since I was probably in a better position than most to do so. However, Rotary in Ireland had always been careful not to alienate any one community, so this meant I had to tread cautiously. At that time, feelings in both communities were divided and bitter, as members of the security forces and prison officers were being attacked or killed on a regular basis, and republicans were being murdered by secret loyalist groups.

So, I met with a retired Protestant minister who had, some years earlier, secretly arranged a meeting with the leadership of the IRA (Irish Republican Army) to discuss peace terms. He invited me to his house in Belfast, where he explained that his discussions with the IRA representative had been disclosed, despite having been in a secret location, and that this had put a stop to the whole initiative. He said, however, that he was prepared to try again.

Some years later, the same minister joined in talks with the local Catholic clergy that ended up in an agreement. Eventually, many years after that, a major peace agreement was accomplished in Northern Ireland. I am convinced that, with a little more effort, this outcome could have been achieved earlier, saving thousands of lives over the ensuing years. But there is absolutely no point in looking backwards. What must be recognised is that, though this initiative, a lot of good was achieved by people who simply wanted to make a difference. I am proud of the work carried out by the members of the TABU committee, as it proved that major results can be achieved when people step out of their comfort zone and believe in themselves. Every one of us has the potential within ourselves to make a difference—more than we can possibly imagine.

The legacy of Martin McGuinness

Martin McGuinness, who passed away in March 2017, was an Irish republican politician who, as a member of the Irish political group Sinn Féin, became the Deputy First Minister for Northern Ireland. He occupied this post for ten years, and earlier in his life he had been the chief of staff of the Irish Republican Army, which made him a wanted man by the UK security forces.

Working alongside US Special Envoy George Mitchell, McGuinness went on to become one of the main architects of the Good Friday Agreement, which formally cemented the peace process in Northern Ireland. With the First Minister, Democratic Unionist Party (DUP) leader Dr. Ian Paisley, the historical agreement would see different political parties sharing power in Northern Ireland.

In 2017, former US President Bill Clinton travelled to Ireland for the funeral of Martin McGuinness. Clinton had played a pivotal role in the Good Friday Agreement as it was he who had appointed George Mitchell to assist in talks between the nationalist and unionist factions, and encouraged the leaders of Northern Ireland's parties to secure the 1998 peace agreement. During his address to the mourners and political representatives who had gathered to pay their respects to the former Deputy First Minister, President Clinton quoted the following, to sum up the contribution of Martin McGuinness:

> "He expanded the definition of *"us"* and shrunk the definition of *"them."*

This quotation resonated with me as I felt it was a very important statement. In today's world, it is all too easy for *us* to judge *them* based on preconceived opinions and bias. So I say, let's bring *us* closer to *them*. Miracles can happen.

Photograph of butterfly by the author

When love conquers everything

Shortly after the fall of communism in Bulgaria, we went on our annual holiday to ski in the mountains with a group of Irish people, as we always did. On one particularly memorable trip, we got chatting to a couple from Northern Ireland each evening at the hotel "après ski" (the social get-together after a day on the slopes.)

George and Catriona (whose names have been changed in order to respect their privacy) told us that, because they were from different religions and backgrounds, they had been unable to marry in Northern Ireland. George explained that he was a Protestant, from a loyalist area, and that his girlfriend was a Catholic from South Armagh. The result was that both families were totally against their marriage. Catriona said it was proving much too difficult and stressful to even consider a wedding in Northern Ireland.

We were in a local village about twenty kilometres from the mountain resort, having dinner with friends, when George and Catriona told us this story. They also said that prior to going on holiday they had considered getting married abroad, if it were at all possible. I took our host aside and quietly asked if he thought such a ceremony might be possible in his country. He thought for a while and said that the local Orthodox priest lived in the same building, and slipped out of our party to go downstairs to enquire. When he returned, he announced that the marriage could take place the very next evening!

I turned to the couple to ask them if they wanted to be married the next day. George proposed to Catriona there and then. It was so romantic and such a special moment that I will never forget. I didn't even hear Catriona's response, but in a few minutes the couple were kissing and I knew that the wedding was on.

The following day, we went skiing as usual, but at lunchtime, Catriona went off to a little shop in the village and bought a dress. That evening we went to the local church with all the people from our ski group. The venue was magical, the bride looked amazing and George asked me to take the wedding pictures and also handed me his video recorder to record the happy event. I thought I ought to say a few words during the ceremony to note such a special occasion for the couple and their friends as, naturally, the service was in Bulgarian. This was the only time I was the wedding photographer and delivered the wedding sermon! I spoke to all present about how love transcends everything and conquers all, even the religious and political divide in Northern Ireland.

The wedding party returned to the hotel and we all reflected on the beautiful and meaningful day we had been so fortunate to have shared. As you can imagine, I have attended thousands of weddings in my long career as a professional photographer, but this incredible ceremony in a little village in the Bulgarian mountains, close to the Greek border, will stand out in my mind forever.

Some years later, I received a phone call from George, who asked if he could book my photography services for his "public" wedding. Needless to say, I was surprised. He explained that attitudes had changed regarding mixed marriages in Northern Ireland so it was finally acceptable for the couple to marry.

Incidentally, I wasn't aware that the Bulgarian wedding had remained a secret from both families all that time and almost gave the game away. I had just started to say how unusual it was to be attending the second wedding of the same couple, when the bride shushed me before I could finish my sentence!

CHAPTER 7

DIFFERENCES AND SIMILARITIES

Portraits of religious leaders in Ireland

While I was running my photography business, I was one of the founding members of the Irish Portrait Group. This was comprised of a small group of professional photographers throughout the country who had come together to advance the craft of fine portraiture and to extend the boundaries of this art. We met regularly in order to educate ourselves further, share experiences and expand our knowledge and set ourselves projects which were judged and critiqued by our peers and experts in the art world.

One of the projects we set ourselves involved undertaking a portrait assignment of a high profile subject of our choosing. I decided my subject would be the leader of the Catholic Church across the whole of Ireland at that time, Cardinal Tomás Ó Fiaich. Ó Fiaich was quite a controversial figure, as he was very open about his political leanings, and held strong republican views. While waiting to hear whether the cardinal would agree to sit for his portrait, as a backup I had also contacted another well-known and controversial religious figure at the time, the Reverend Dr. Ian Paisley, a Protestant religious leader and politician.

In 1971, Ian Paisley had founded and led the Democratic Unionist Party, the largest political party in Northern Ireland. He was also head of his own Protestant, fundamentalist church, the Free Presbyterian Church of Ulster. Many years later, he would become the First Minister of Northern

Ireland as a result of the peace process, which saw a settlement between the IRA, all political parties and the governments of Southern Ireland and the United Kingdom. He was, particularly at the time I was meeting him, a figure of hate for all republicans as he was the leader of Loyalism in Northern Ireland. To say that Paisley was very anti-republican is an understatement.

To my surprise, both men agreed to my request, so I decided to do two portraits. I arranged an appointment for the same day—in the morning with Dr. Paisley in Belfast at his church and at the Armagh home of Cardinal Ó Fiaich in the afternoon.

This was a very tense time, as rarely did Southern Irish, republican Catholics mix with Northern Irish loyalists. There was a great mistrust of each other, as so many atrocities had been committed up to that point by both sides—the IRA on one, and extreme loyalists on the other. People were being shot on an almost daily basis and the commercial centres of Belfast and other cities and towns were being bombed, causing severe destruction and loss of life. Catholics and republicans were perceived as supporters of the IRA and when I arranged the meeting, Dr. Paisley was identified as being very extreme in this regard, but I was assured by his private secretary that I would be respected and in no danger.

On arrival, I introduced myself to Dr. Paisley as being from the South of Ireland and, since my name is Gaelic for John, he would not have been under any doubt that I was a Catholic. I decided to set up my lights at his preaching lectern and set to work on his portrait. During the session, I told him where I was going that afternoon, and that I had an appointment to undertake a portrait of the cardinal. He laughed nervously. I asked if they had ever met and he said they had not. I was amazed at this answer as Northern Ireland is such a small place—measuring about 135 kilometres (85 miles) north to south and about 175 kilometres (110 miles) east to west, which is about one-sixth of the total area of the island of Ireland. These leaders had, many times, scorned each other in television studios, but didn't know each other at all!

After I had finished the assignment, Dr. Paisley presented me with a religious book that he had written, based on the bible. He proceeded to address it to me on the inside cover, which is usual for an author when gifting their work to someone. However, I noticed that he had begun to write my name with the English spelling, *Shaun*, I explained that my Christian name was in fact the Gaelic version, *Sean*. He said that he had never written anything in Irish. This was the extent of the divide in Ireland between people at that time—Irish Gaelic was a foreign language to him. A lot of bridges would need building and a lot of hearts and minds would have to be opened to love and understanding.

So, unbelievably, Dr. Paisley agreed to write my name in Irish in his book that day—the first time that he had ever done so. At that moment, I really felt that a bridge had been built and crossed. I also think that the fact that Irish language classes would eventually be organised and attended by Protestants in East Belfast is nothing short of a miracle.

My afternoon appointment with Cardinal Tomás Ó Fiaich, Primate of All Ireland, took place in his home in Armagh city. Armagh is the ecclesiastical capital of Ireland and is very close to where I was brought up in County Monaghan, although my home was across the border in Southern Ireland. During his sitting, I explained to the cardinal where I had been that morning and told him that I had been very surprised to discover that he and Dr. Paisley had never met. He had no comment, other than a nervous laugh.

The day ended well and, I must say, both the reverend and the cardinal were perfect gentlemen and treated me with respect. Soon after this, Cardinal Ó Fiaich attended an exhibition of my photography and Dr. Paisley used the portraits I took of him for various publications and CD covers, both of which felt like a real honour.

Sometime later, the cardinal made an important visit to a high-security prison in Northern Ireland to consult with republican prisoners. He would play an important role in encouraging the men to come off their historic hunger strike, which prepared the way for an eventual agreement between all parties.

Years later, Dr. Paisley took part in talks between republican and Southern Irish politicians to reach the historic agreement that was brokered directly by President Bill Clinton, US president at the time. The president accompanied the prime minister of the UK, Tony Blair, to Ireland to conclude the Good Friday Agreement. Dr. Paisley played a major part in the talks and was responsible for bringing extreme loyalists to the table. He went on to become First Minster of Northern Ireland, sharing equal power and responsibility with his Deputy First Minister, Martin McGuinness who was an ex-IRA member and leading republican. This was truly a miracle and proof for me that all things are possible in our world.

The great lessons in forgiveness—
the bombing of Enniskillen

In 1989, a large bomb went off in Enniskillen, Northern Ireland, near the town's war memorial during a Remembrance Sunday ceremony to commemorate those military personnel who have died in war. Ten civilians and a police officer were killed. One of the victims was eighteen-year-old student nurse, Marie Wilson. Her father, Gordon Wilson, was a fellow Rotary member in the neighbouring club of Enniskillen, just across the border from the club in Monaghan where I was a member. We learned about the death of Gordon's daughter's from a television news report that evening and were very shocked. However, what happened next was to completely stun us all. Gordon described how he'd been with his daughter when the explosion went off and held her hand as she died beneath the rubble. His words were to have a profound effect across the world, as they were recognised as a manifestation of one of the greatest acts of forgiveness to those who had killed Marie. In the now-famous interview, he spoke of the last words between himself and his dying daughter.

"She held my hand tightly and gripped me as hard as she could. She said, 'Daddy, I love you very much.' Those were her exact words to me, and those were the last words I ever heard her say. But I bear no ill. I bear no grudge. Dirty sort of talk is not going to bring her back to life. She was a great wee lassie. She loved her profession. She was a pet. She's dead. She's in heaven and we shall meet again. I will pray for these men tonight and every night."

These words may be among the most remembered from the decades of conflict in Northern Ireland, uttered by an ordinary, yet extraordinary man. He also begged that no-one take revenge for Marie's death and pleaded with loyalists not to do so.

I went to meet George Wilson some time later, when I was establishing our special committee, and it was a pleasure to meet someone who was able to forgive, in such an unexpected way, the people who killed his daughter just hours after the terrible event. People like this live on in the spirit of humanity to lead us to great heights. Gordon joined his daughter in 1995 when he passed away following a heart attack. After the Enniskillen bomb, he had worked as a peace campaigner, holding meetings with members of Sinn Féin, loyalist paramilitaries and once with the Provisional IRA, in an attempt to persuade them to abandon violence.

I heard American philosopher, author and speaker, Dr. Wayne Dyer, talk about forgiveness and he quoted the following, beautiful words attributed to Mark Twain. This really resonated with me about forgiving people who I had perceived had wronged me.

> "Forgiveness is the fragrance the violet sheds on the heel that has crushed it."

My mosque

I am perhaps the only Irish native to own a mosque!

This came about when I was the landlord of a large house that I rented to the local Islamic Society in the town of Cavan. They had converted the house to use as a mosque, which I was perfectly happy about, as they were good people. Because there was one large room in the house, they decided it would be suitable for praying, so they made markings for the direction for prayer and displayed the Koran there. On Fridays, the mosque was full, but people came each day to pray and young children were there all day on Saturday. Whenever I called to repair something in the house, I felt a great sense of peace inside and, in fact, I used to pray there when I was alone.

When I had the opportunity, I enjoyed chatting with the leader about the various aspects of the Islamic religion and, on occasion, I was invited to join them for a meal. During these times we discussed the role of Muhammad while he was on earth, and I discovered that his role was similar to that of Jesus in my religion, who I believe to have been a great prophet on earth.

It was very unusual to have a working mosque in a small town like Cavan. After all, this was Ireland, where the major religion was Catholic, with a mix of Protestants in each town.

I have learned throughout my life that people of different religions and cultures are essentially the same. It is too easy to put labels on people (something that I have been guilty of myself) but by meeting people from different walks of life and communicating with them, we can come to understand their beliefs, and begin to see similarities rather than differences. I believe that the majority of members of all organizations and religions are genuinely good people, and that it is unfortunate that there are other, misguided souls who become extremists.

I learned this through my experiences with members of the Muslim community and the different religious groups of Northern Ireland, as well as by meeting and working with those from other cultures internationally.]

Just by speaking to people all bridges can be crossed

"Faith is a rope which you hold in this world and in the next. (89X-261)"
(from *Prophet of Our Times: The Life and Teachings of Peter Deunov* by David Lorimer)

Photograph taken by the author

The Russian experience

After the economic crash of 2008 in Ireland, we were inundated by Irish owners of overseas holiday properties who were desperate to find buyers. Most were under great pressure to sell their investment properties abroad as the Irish economy entered severe recession.

This was how our company was founded—we formed specifically to do this. My business partner and I travelled to Russia to meet and organize agents there who would find buyers for the properties of struggling Irish owners. We considered this a real opportunity for those Irish owners who had invested in properties in Bulgaria, Turkey and Spain, as the Russians were buying up properties in these areas.

So in November 2009 we travelled to Moscow, then on to St. Petersburg by train, where we stayed for a night. We had planned to return to Moscow the following day but as we waited on the high-speed Nevsky Express train, the news came through that it had been blown up during a terrorist attack as it left from Moscow. The bomb had exploded under the train, causing it to derail. Twenty-seven people lost their lives and almost one hundred were injured.

We were able to catch a later train back to Moscow, but we both realised how fortunate we had been. When you have had a close escape such as this, you really appreciate every moment and are thankful for the opportunities that each day brings.

I am always grateful for the protection of my angels.

Photograph of Lake in Cootehill taken by the author

CHAPTER 8

DEVELOPMENTS — UNWELCOME AND WELCOME

In the last chapter I explained that, along with my business partner, I had established an overseas property consultancy firm to help Irish holiday homeowners trying to sell their properties abroad. Sadly, the business ran into serious difficulties and had to be liquidated in 2015, causing major problems for our clients, many of whom were owed money. Understandably, they pursued us with vigour. This was a very trying time for all concerned and, unfortunately, problems continue to the present day.

The experience changed me a lot as a person, as it required me to shed all former preconceptions and deal with new realities. I had to become stronger and seek help from various sources on a daily basis. I changed, or rather, I believe that I travelled closer to my true self—my soul self. During this challenging period, I discovered self-help books by several authors, including Dr. Wayne Dyer, to be extremely helpful. In particular, I found Anita Moorjani's book, *Dying to by Me*, inspiring; it described her struggle with cancer, her near-death experience and eventual healing. Also, Immaculée Ilibagiza's book, *Left to Tell*, is the harrowing but uplifting story of her suffering and survival during the Rwandan massacres, which saw her family brutally murdered. Becoming more aware of the near-death experiences and significant endurances suffered by these people helped me to keep going. I began to shed any egotistical concerns and stop worrying about what people would think of me, as court cases against me became public knowledge. Because there were so many irate clients, I faced the possibility of imprisonment. All this is still unresolved, but what is certain is that I have lost a large part of my former ego and discovered a more pure, spiritual self. I have begun to love myself more and stop blaming myself for past mistakes. Eventually, I took the huge step of being thankful for all the turmoil in my life, as I have come to recognise that it is helping me to fulfil my life's purpose, which has greatly assisted in my spiritual development.

However, my main concern was about putting my family through turmoil, so I tried to shield them from the extent of my problems. I feared it would cause too much worry for them and, naively, thought that I could resolve the situation in a short time. I realise now that this was a huge mistake— but thankfully my family are proving to be a lot stronger than I could ever have hoped. I now believe that I cannot keep beating myself up about the situation and must find the best way to keep going forward.

I am therefore writing this book openly and honestly, so that it may assist those who also find themselves faced with adversity. I believe that the purpose of my journey is to help them realise that, just as my life has been enriched by challenges, they too will have the opportunity to develop on their own path.

In other words, I wish to share the lessons I have learned so far in life.

The Turkish experience

As problems with clients grew increasingly serious, I travelled to Turkey to finish some business there. On the plane journey, I was guided to visit the House of the Virgin Mary near Ephesus.

The House of Mary is a place of pilgrimage where the mother of Jesus is believed to have lived out her final years. My visit there was quite an experience. As there was no public transport to the site, I arranged for a young man to take me there on his moped, or motorcycle, up the mountain road to the house which is almost seven kilometres (four miles) out of Ephesus. The building is now a small, Christian church. I discovered that my driver, who lived locally, was Muslim and had never visited the site before. I left him outside and noticed he had started to pray as I entered the small building. The church was empty apart from two other people, and visitors were being instructed by a young nun to walk straight through to an exit at the top end of the church. To my left I noticed a lady crying on a church kneeler. I saw a vacant kneeler to the right and went over to it and knelt down to pray. A surge of emotion came over me as I asked for help with my difficult situation back home. I spoke from the heart and beseeched Mary to help me. Totally unexpectedly, I began to cry. I was totally overwhelmed with emotion and felt an intense presence of love.

I don't know how long I stayed there, crying, but I received a clear message from Mary saying that she would protect me and my family. This was what I had been praying for since entering the little church. Once again, it is difficult to explain the experience, but it was such a clear message—as if someone physically kneeling beside me had just uttered the words.

I got up to leave and when I passed the young nun, she spoke.

"Mary loves you very much. She is happy you came here to pray."

I felt then that this nun was a very special person, as she was so positive and open. Even her eyes seemed to speak to me. We hugged each other and I thanked her and left.

When I approached my Muslim "taxi", who was outside waiting on me, I was still crying. However, these were not tears of sadness, but of an overwhelming emotion that I am unable to explain exactly; I just know that I felt an experience so strong that it couldn't be physically absorbed into my body. However, I felt able to absorb this emotion into my spiritual being, where it still resides; it is an inexplicable part of me, but is of immense comfort during challenging times. So I drew upon this help offered to me by Mary during my business difficulties, and I now have a much closer relationship with Mary and her son Jesus, in a very practical way.

My driver took me back on his motorcycle to a bus stop just over twenty kilometres away (twelve miles) where he tried to overcharge me. But I forgave him for that!

Dealing with anger

In the same way I forgave that young man, I sent love and healing to those clients who had attacked me in any way, due to our business losing their money. Some sent intimidating texts and phone calls, others threatened me with physical attack, and some sent "tough boys" to my house on their behalf. It was disturbing at the time, but my feelings of love were reciprocated when I sent this to them, along with gold light and healing.

When I was sending out these feelings of love and healing, I naturally did so to my wife and children also, as well as to a cousin who had been given only three months to live. Thanks to the healing power of Jesus and Mary she had many years of happiness before she eventually passed over. Although I don't believe that we need to follow a particular religion, I feel very close to Mary and Jesus and sometimes call upon their healing power.

Many times, when I travelled to meet former clients who had lost money through our company, I broke down and cried in front of them when explaining how I had tried everything to get their money back. This was not through fear or self-pity, but rather a deeper emotion that came from somewhere within my soul. When I told clients that I would do everything in my power to make it right for them, I meant it sincerely—as I could feel their pain.

However, to be honest, I must admit that there were times when I felt that, for everyone's sake, it would be easier for me to take my own life and be done with it all.

Once in 2016, I had arranged to meet with a client in person and, just beforehand, I was guided to go to the men's room to give myself some time to prepare for what I knew would be a difficult encounter. When I closed the door behind me, I was aware of something in my jacket pocket; I put my hand inside and discovered a holy image of Mary with the infant Jesus. I held it and asked them for protection and, even though the meeting that followed was indeed a difficult one, and once again I broke down, I knew that I had been protected. Despite the client's harsh words, I felt a huge degree of empathy and strength and told him that I could totally appreciate his frustration, and stayed calm and honest. Afterwards, I thanked Jesus and Mary.

In most cases, I sought to meet with my business clients in person in order to seek a resolution that was acceptable to them. I recall a particular meeting with three people, at my own request, after which I had planned to meet with the author Anita Moorejani. Anita is someone who I greatly admire and she had travelled from the US to speak to a delegation in Dublin. Unfortunately, my meeting with the clients left me so distraught that I couldn't go to her presentation. I now regret this, as I believe it was a mistake not to have gone to meet this inspirational woman.

Of all the challenges presented by the problems in our business, the one that I found the most difficult involved explaining to a family member how his money had been lost in the venture. I had always been close to this person, having played together as children and shared our lives completely when growing up. I remember so well when, at around eighteen years of age, he had emigrated to Australia; I think that this was the first time that I had experienced an acute feeling of loneliness.

Mistakenly, I had put off telling this family member about the loss of the company but, when the situation inevitably came to light, I had to face up to him and explain everything. I had agonised over this for a long time and asked from my heart for help in resolving the situation in some way. I was confident that I would get this help.

I went on to explain what had happened and, naturally, he was upset with me, just as I was disappointed with myself. I abandoned all sense of ego and told him that he had every right to point out my mistakes, because I had failed him. I opened myself up, broke down completely and apologised profusely, explaining that my motives had always been good. I admitted that the mistakes that I had made had caused financial difficulties for him and others, which had left me agonizing for a long time about what to do. After admitting to him that I had contemplated suicide on several occasions, I remember crying out, hyperventilating, and running out of the house. I remained outside alone in my car, sobbing, for a time. I realise now that I probably should not have been driving in that state of mind. However, once I had recovered sufficient composure to be able to concentrate, I drove myself back home.

I honestly think that the physical release I experienced through abandoning myself to the universe, in all that shouting and crying, may have been what saved me. I hadn't realised how much stress had been bottled up inside over the years, as I battled with the company's problems and tried, in vain, to find solutions.

To my amazement, the next morning he rang me and said that money wasn't everything in this world, and that I should take care of myself and my health. It is difficult to find the words to describe how much this response meant to me. I believe that, by asking, I was given the strength to be my real self, which in turn enabled me to be open and to respond to the situation in a totally honest way with my family.

Mother Theresa was a completely egoless and great person. When asked once what she said when praying, she replied, "I listen." When asked how God responded to her prayers, she said, "He listens."

By taking account of all the good things in life, either by writing them down or stating them aloud, our attitude to life can change immediately, and this has a consequence on how we live. For example, if we say thanks for the simple things such as fresh air, food, good health, family support, appreciation, and so on, it can make a massive difference in our mood. In fact, as it causes certain neural circuits to be activated, creating feelings of contentment, gratitude could be considered a natural antidepressant.

Holding your own hand

I was attending a mindfulness course a few years ago, when a young woman surprised everyone there when she told us that she wrote down three things for which she felt grateful every day. I must say, this wisdom in one so young impressed myself and everyone else at the time.

During the same course, in one of the meditation sessions, the leader asked us to become aware of our bodies and the positions of our limbs. When she got to the hands and asked us to consider their positions, I had one hand loosely linked to the other, which I consider a normal position. However, I began to feel something quite extraordinary, as if my left hand was holding the right in a loving and supportive way. It sounds strange, but it felt really beautiful—as if I was being supported and was really holding my own hand.

During the feedback session afterwards, we were asked to state one thing we felt that we had got from the course. I said, "I learned to hold my own hand." I must say, everyone became quite emotional at that point, including me.

Now, when feeling in need of reassurance, I simply hold my own hand and feel comforted, as if my higher being is looking after my vulnerable or concerned self. This is an exercise I recommend trying. After all, there is nothing to lose—but so much, potentially, to gain.

Photograph taken by the author

CHAPTER 9

TRAUMATIC EVENTS AND HEALING

On 21st March, 2016, my family and I received a terrible fright when we heard a loud hammering on the front and back doors of our house simultaneously. Up until then, we had led very quiet lives. We had always been hard-working, law-abiding people; I provided for my family as best I could through my professional photography business, brought a service to the community and did my best to provide help to those in need wherever possible. So you can imagine my horror when I opened to door to discover four members of the police force demanding entry to our home.

It transpired that our clients had filed complaints against our overseas property company following its liquidation, and that they had transferred those complaints against me, personally. It was understandable that the irate clients had reacted with such vigour, since they, along with many others in Ireland at that time, had found themselves faced with significant financial difficulties.

The police later explained that, upon receiving complaints of this nature, they were obliged to investigate the situation, which had ultimately led to the traumatic visit. They said that the police officers had been dispatched from Dublin to question me and search the house for any company records or business papers. I was extremely concerned about the effect all this was having on my family but, I must admit, my wife showed a strength that I don't think even she knew she possessed until we were faced with this situation. Because there were four officers, we felt very intimidated at the time but, looking back, I see now that they were only doing their job. They searched the house, took computers, phones, and all company records and announced that they were arresting me and that I was to accompany them to Dublin for questioning.

Before leaving with the police officers, I hugged my family tightly and felt a special bond of support. En route to Dublin, I broke down and cried. When I composed myself, there was a lighter moment when I asked if I could keep my Kindle to read. The police officers were amused and one said that he'd never come across anyone in my situation requesting a Kindle before.

When we arrived in the city, I was put in a cell. I prayed hard for support during this harrowing experience, asking my ancestors, my angels and Mother Mary and Jesus for their help. I drew upon the memory of my experience at the house of Mary in Turkey, when her "voice" told me that she would protect me and my family. My prayers were answered and I had another experience in the police station just before questioning began. I felt a presence I knew was Mary and was surrounded by her light. It stayed with me all that day and during the harrowing night that followed.

I was finally released at 3.30am the next morning and was asked to present myself at another police station two days later for further questioning, which I did. I was again put in a cell and I noticed some graffiti on the floor. The words *Paul is with me*, were written in ink on the wooden floorboards. As soon as I read this, a voice deep inside said, "Ask who is with you." I did and a moment later I received an answer.

It turned out that the voice was that of a relative who had passed on many years earlier. For that reason, I had not thought of her in a very long time, my great-aunt on my mother's side who we had known as Aunt Bridget. She was a nun and had always been a very quiet, unassuming person, and full of great love for everyone. I could see her image very clearly, smiling as always. Her presence had a very calming effect on me in a very beautiful way. She was very close to me that day, and has remained so ever since.

I must point out that I was never mistreated by any of the officers who came to my house or who subsequently questioned me at the stations. There were merely reacting as instructed during such investigations. I was allowed to return home.

Dark thoughts

A civil court case was taken against me as a result of our former clients' complaints. At the time, one of the most difficult outcomes for me was the thought of the resulting publicity surrounding the case. I knew that the events would be reported in the media the day after the hearing. Journalists and local news reporters would say that I had been called to court because I'd been accused of wrongdoing towards clients, as a result of the company's past activities. To say I was devastated is an understatement; I had spent my whole life building up my reputation and had always been conscious of how I was perceived by the public. Such accusations were extremely hurtful, but my main concern was how this would affect my family when they heard about the case on local radio. I was particularly concerned for my wife, as her family reputation was very important to her and I couldn't bear the thought that people from her small hometown would soon learn about the whole affair.

I was in a very dark place and didn't know what to do. On my way home from the proceedings, I decided to call with a hypnotherapist, a very good friend and talented business and professional coach, as well as a gifted intuitive. I told her of my situation and described how devastated I was, not for myself, but for my family.

My friend could tell that I was I having suicidal thoughts and comforted me by pointing out that there were worse things than a court case. She said that lots of peoples' situations changed every day, but life still went on. Yes, naturally the locals would talk when the news came out, but she assured me that within a few days, someone or something else would be the topic of conversation. My friend said that the most important thing to consider at present was my mental well-being. When I expressed my concerns about my wife, she pointed out that my wife would learn to cope, just as I would.

From that point onwards, I began the process of adopting a more positive outlook on my situation. I decided to continue life as usual, going out in public in my hometown. I admit this was definitely not easy as, once the news broke, I felt that people I met in the street were looking at me, and passing judgement. However, some of my family members and close friends called me after the radio report about my court case, and it is impossible to describe my relief at their offers of support. It meant so much to hear them say that their thoughts were with me.

Because I had the support and love of family and friends, I felt that I could gradually let go of my concerns about what others thought of me. This was such a relief and it opened my heart in an amazingly liberating way.

Yes, I still have moments when dark feelings creep into my head, but I am working through this, with much more acceptance of consequences. I am confident that these extremely testing times have both strengthened me mentally and enlightened me spiritually.

Suicide is never an answer

Although I have experienced the direct effects of suicide on a family after my brother's death, I have to admit that during my times of great darkness caused by my business problems, I had considered the notion that suicide would be welcome, as it would be much easier to drift off into the next world.

However, I have eventually come to the conclusion that it is not the answer. There are two reasons for this:

Firstly, we must consider the devastation that suicide will cause our loved ones; despite what we think, taking our life will not make theirs easier.

Secondly, our feelings change with time—sometimes as quickly as from one hour to the next. Active feelings of suicide are often temporary. We must ask ourselves: Is it really the life we are living that we want to end, and not that we want to end our life? Is there another way to solve our problems? Can we seek help? Very often, solutions can occur unexpectedly to problems that had previously seemed unsolvable. Even if a solution is not immediately apparent, acknowledgement of the situation and realising that we need to seek help will dramatically improve our situation.

I remember back then, that the words of the following song by Kris Kristofferson kept playing in my head. These lines would come to me as soon as I woke up and they continued at intervals throughout the day.

Come and lay down by my side
Till the early mornin' light
All I'm takin' is your time
Help me make it through the night
I don't care what's right or wrong
I don't try to understand
Let the devil take tomorrow
Lord, tonight I need a friend
Yesterday is dead and gone
And tomorrow's out of sight
And it's sad to be alone
Help me make it through the night
Kris Kristofferson

To have reached the conclusion about suicide was difficult, after having had such dark thoughts for so long. I could never have come to this decision, that it was not the answer to my problems, on my own. I received a lot of help from loved ones, reached out to the universe and, despite what some people were saying, discovered that I was not bad— in fact, I learned that I was good and full of God's love. I also forgave those who, I felt back then, were causing my family and I such anxiety.

Finally, I faced myself, decided to hold my head up in public and stopped worrying about what people thought.

All this led to a complete change in me. I learned how to live and be happy in the present moment, how to appreciate the value of the love I had received, and would continue to receive, from those closest to me. I discovered how to trust in the help that was available.

Before, I used to look at others going about their daily lives, seemingly free of all worries except those of the everyday nature. I wished that I could be "normal" like them and, despite the love of close family, I felt that I was vilified by the world because of my potentially hopeless situation.

When I started to live in the present, all this changed. I began to celebrate what I had, rather than complaining about what I hadn't got: I had food on the table, my health, the love of my family, my skills… in other words, I had life. Each day, as I relaxed more and continued to trust and rely on the help that I was receiving, I learned to cope and sort out some of the difficulties, dealing with them one at a time. I began to become my true self. Eventually, I learned how to let go of negative thoughts and stopped worrying about situations that might never happen. For the first time in years I felt a sense of freedom and realised the extent of my distress due to business problems.

> "The presence of fear means you are relying on your own strength."

The above is a line from the book *A Course in Miracles*, by Helen Schucman. I found it to be a very profound statement, as I believe fear is the opposite of love. Naturally, we all suffer from fear or anxiety at some point in our life, to varying degrees. However, now I know that it is possible to gradually lessen this suffering and eventually eliminate it altogether. I am presently on that journey.

Firstly, we must be aware that fear can be controlled. This is an important and totally necessary step because, it is only when we realise this that we can begin to progress towards our goals each day, allowing us to start letting go of fear.

I have come to realise that in taking positive steps and releasing both fear and the ego, so much can be achieved. More importantly, no matter how distressing or disturbing a situation becomes, with the support of the universe and the help of good people, life becomes tolerable and we can begin to envisage an end to our problems.

While researching this book, I bought *The Courage to be Creative* by Doreen Virtue. Within the chapters, there is one that I found very interesting, titled, "The Courage to Bring Your Shadows into the Light", in which the author urges people to face their feelings— even those about which they don't feel very proud. In other words, life is about having the courage to embrace every aspect of yourself. This is what I began to do, and what I continue to strive to do.

I once heard Dr. Wayne Dyer speaking on Hay House Radio about the changes he experienced after having been diagnosed with cancer. He said that he had been healed by Saint John of God, with the use of herbs and distant healing. I felt that he was speaking to me directly when we he said that, at some stage, he had learned to let go of his fear about his condition. He explained that, once you let go of fear, the only substitute is love and said that when he allowed love to take over his fear, he was cured. In fact, Anita Moorjani, said something similar. The speaker and award-winning writer who had a near-death experience explained that when she had released the fear about her cancer and substituted this with love, she had been cured.

I have let go of the massive fear I held to some extent, but it is something that I am still working on.

Visitations

On Easter Saturday night, March 16th, I had a very clear message through what may have been a dream, but was so real for me that I have never forgotten it. In fact, I remember every detail.

In this dream, a stranger approached me and offered to take me down a ski slope, extremely fast. They said that we could go directly down the steepest slope, in a straight line rather than with turns. I asked why on earth we would want to do that, since we would be unable to see what lay ahead during our descent, since the mountain was almost vertical in parts. This person responded by telling me that I had to trust them. I suddenly felt a close attachment to them, and became certain that they would lead the way down safely. Then, stars began to shine in front of me and all around me, and the person said that I was now protected. At that instant, I realised that this was an angel and that I would be completely safe, despite my difficulties. At the same time, I realised that it wasn't necessary for me to see angels to know that they would be protecting me. I felt that now they would be moving with me, almost as though they were part of my being. I woke up knowing that this was real and that I had just been visited by angels. I had received a profound message just when I really needed it— during one of the most trying weeks of my life. From now on, I knew that I would receive guidance and help on every step of my journey.

Two days later, during a forest walk, I asked who had come to me and who it was who had guided me in such a way. I received the answer that this person had been an angel, Archangel Michael, to be precise. When I returned home, I discovered one of my angel cards face-up on a desk in the kitchen. It featured the Archangel Michael and the message written on it was, "Pay attention to your dreams." I went into another room to find a second card from Archangel Michael that read, "Sit back and relax and allow the situation to naturally unfold."

I realised that the message had been given to me by the Archangel Michael using the skiing analogy as I would understand this immediately, having skied in Bulgaria for many years. The sport had also provided me with a lot of inspiration and helped me have the courage to achieve what, on occasion, had seemed practically impossible.

Throughout this time, I had been sending healing light to my former business partner, asking the angels and Jesus to give him courage and to help him achieve success in his life. I believe that this is an important practice, as it frees you up and removes you from any negative blame, thereby allowing everyone to move forward in love.

I was also greatly influenced by the book, *Whatever Arrives, Love That,* by Matt Khan, in which he offers an important message. He claims that, essentially, no matter what confronts you, in terms of the difficulties you have to face, if you go through it with love, you will have a completely new perspective on problems and trials of your life.

Five ways to change your life forever

Because of the business challenges I have faced, I am sometimes asked to give motivational talks to groups of people. Regardless of whether they are small, intimate workshops or large gatherings, I always propose the following five points of action as a good way to initiate change:

1. Let go of control and surrender yourself to each day: "Let go and let God."
2. Change thinking and acting from head to heart.
3. Ask for higher guidance each day in all your actions.
4. Mediate (even for a short time) each day and let go of your thinking.
5. Be grateful for the good things you have in life and think of these often.

Wayne Dyer and so many other authors and broadcasters have said that it is extremely important—more important than we will ever realise, to have gratitude for the good things we have in life, as this allows us to begin a whole new, positive way of thinking.

When I was promoting the aims of the Rotary Committee through our *Mutual Understanding* project in Ireland and worldwide, I was, in a non-religious sense, greatly influenced by this prayer of Saint Francis:

> *Make me a channel of your peace*
> *Where there's despair in life, let me bring hope,*
> *Where there is darkness, only light,*
> *And where there's sadness, ever joy.*

When we help others to find peace and love, we are also, in a hugely important way, helping ourselves. When we sow love, we are reaping great love for ourselves, repaid tenfold. This is probably the only time when we can feel alright about being selfish and anticipate the blessings that we will receive, because it is a win-win situation for all concerned.

I once saw a newspaper headline, in the sports section, referring to an Irish football team manager; the words emphasized what I thought was an extremely important message for us all:

> "It is not enough to want to win. We need to feel it."

When we set our intention to achieve, whether it be in business, spiritual achievement, happiness, peace or love, if we can *feel* what we desire, we are almost there. In fact, we are there; we just need to wait and let it happen. It is then we "Let go and let God."

I have discovered that, through challenging times, we progress in every way. We receive great gifts of insight, patience, understanding, empathy for others and a realisation of our unimaginable gifts and strengths. These are truly great blessings to receive.

Naturally, the last thing I ever wanted in business were the problems that I encountered. However, I am now able to thank God that I have been faced with such trails (at least, I am a lot of the time, anyway) It can be difficult to reach that particular mind-set, but I consider it a work in progress. We must strive to rise above our problems, try our best to solve them, learn how to trust in resolutions that are best for everyone, then learn from our experience, grow and move on.

I found the following quote from philosopher and spiritual teacher, Peter Deunov, very pertinent, although not always easy to accept...

> "Human happiness is defined by the hardships and conflicts you have been through. The greater they are, the greater your happiness."

I once heard someone say, "We can only think of one thing at a time, so if you are becoming overwhelmed with fear or worry, think of a good thought instead." This is also sound advice. I used to feel that it wasn't possible to do this, that I needed to stay focussed on a problem until I found a resolution. I would feel guilty if I stopped trying to fix things. But it is a fact that answers often present themselves and new ways of thinking arrive when we relax a little and ask the universe tor help.

There have been many times in the last few years when I could not see any resolution to the problems I faced. I became overwhelmed and dropped to my knees and simply cried out to God and the universe for help. In doing this, I learned to completely let go of trying to solve everything myself and implored for assistance. This letting go and relying on trust can help us achieve so much, as it opens us up to our higher self and solutions begin to arrive. This applies whether the problems are considered minor, such as losing something or failing an exam, or major issues, such as loss of one's livelihood, having one's freedom taken away, or the death of a loved one. I am learning that people have inside them the potential for great resilience; when required, we can be much more capable than we ever thought possible.

Those who have come back from near-death experience all reiterate, on returning from their journey to 'the other side', the notion that we are part of the universe, and that it places amazing resources at our disposal. Indeed, Dr. Wayne Dyer was reflecting on the power of the universe through his words, which I have paraphrased here, "Who makes all the flowers bloom?" This is pertinent if we reflect on how the human body develops and grows, and the synchronicity in nature and in the bird and animal kingdom.

Wayne Dyer also said, "When we change the way we look at things, the things we look at change." I find this an amazing statement, as it suggests that when we shift our thoughts from the negative to the positive and look at life with enthusiasm, our life adapts accordingly and we receive gifts and opportunities beyond our dreams. This is the path I have started on and intend to follow from now on.

Trust that something will happen

I really enjoyed listening to a radio interview with Sir Paul McCartney a few years ago, during which he described difficult times in his life, and in particular when The Beatles were breaking up. He said that the group members all had one very simple philosophy and often quoted it when they were facing difficulties. This was the phrase, "Something will happen," He said that it was true, as something always did happen.

I will never forget his explanation of how this mantra originated for the band; one night, early in the band's career, he said that they had been returning to Liverpool from a gig in London in their van. It was very late and they were traveling during a snowstorm, when suddenly their van left the road, slid down a steep embankment and came to a halt at the bottom. They all wondered how they were going to get out of their predicament, as they were miles away from a phone, in the middle of the countryside. One of the band members in the van asked, "So, what will we do now?" and another simply replied, "Something will happen." So they stayed there and waited, totally trusting in this fact. Sure enough, someone eventually appeared from out of the darkness to help them and they were rescued and got home safely. Sir Paul said that after this incident they always quoted that phrase when they were faced with a challenging situation…and something always happened.

A prophet from Bulgaria

While listening to a rebroadcast of one of Dr. Wayne Dyer's programmes on Hay House Radio a couple of years ago, Wayne, who passed away in August 2015, highly recommended the book *Prophet of our Times,* by Peter Lorimer. The subject of this publication was the Bulgarian mystic, Peter Deunov. Wayne had been invited to write the forward for the book, and he said that Peter Deunov, whose spiritual name is Beinsa Douno, was one of the most spiritually important people to have been born on earth over the last one hundred and fifty years. In fact, the following statement was made by the great philosopher Albert Einstein:

> "The whole world bows down before me. I bow down
> before the master, Peter Deunov."

Naturally, because of my close connection with Bulgaria, I was fascinated. I immediately bought the electronic version of *Prophet of our Times*, downloaded it to my ebook reader and began reading it there and then.

I learned that Deunov had lived in Bulgaria from 1864 to 1944. His teachings were simple and direct; he was a prophet who taught the importance of living in love, light, peace and joy. In his teachings, Deunov explained how to find love, wisdom, truth, justice, harmony and balance in life.

As a result, each day I too ask that love, light, peace and joy be all around me, as well as in me. This seems simple, but it has made a remarkable difference to my life.

Artistic inspiration

I was very close to my mother, Kathleen, who passed away at the age of ninety-two. In her later years, she attended art classes and soon became a prolific painter. She often produced landscapes using my photographs, and was inspired by the beauty of the scenery that surrounded her. She may not have known it but she was also a conceptual artist to some extent, and painted with real meaning.

Anyway, today I was clearing out my office space and by pure coincidence (or possibly not) I came across one of her paintings. The work was to celebrate the new millennium and I was amazed to see that she had represented, artistically, the exact teachings of Peter Deunov! She had painted the words *love*, *peace* and *joy,* alongside an image of a burning candle to represent *light*, and a dove for *peace* accompanied by a figure holding a branch as a symbol of nature.

A painting by the author's mother depicting love,
light, peace and joy

The following is just one of many inspirational quotes from Deunov…

> "In the realisation of desires, the law says that you must put it into your subconscious mind and not give it any more thought. Then work in that direction without thinking about when the desire will be realised and what the results will be. Put a seed in the soil and it will show you how to achieve your desires."
>
> (From *Prophet for our Times: The Life and Teachings of Peter Deunov* by David Lorimer)

Deunov often used music and dance as a form of prayer and promoted exercise and diet as a way of enhancing enlightenment. I discovered that I was familiar with many of the locations where he and his followers went to pray. In fact, his disciples still meet on the Rila mountains to dance and pray together. I have walked and skied on this mountain, the scenery of which I find very similar to Switzerland. It is an area that is much loved by many Bulgarian friends, in particular Theodora's father as he is originally from this region, and her grandparents still live in the area.

Photograph of Musala Peak, Rila Mountain, Bulgaria.

Another quote from the teachings of Deunov that I found inspiring...

> "People should know that they are linked with millions of
> other minds on earth and with others not on the earth.
> If that link is harmonious, the results of their lives will be
> good."

Finally, he expresses, "Human thoughts have great power; they penetrate everywhere and change things imperceptibly."

The author of *Prophet for our Times*, David Lorimer, is from the United Kingdom. He studied Bulgarian in order to accurately translate the writings of Peter Deunov to produce this wonderful book. David himself is a most interesting person and a wonderful soul. He is the author and editor of many other books, including R*adical Prince*, the subject of which is the apparent heir to the British throne, Charles, Prince of Wales.

Healing powers

Through numerous trips to Bulgaria, I have found that many people are passionate about health and wellbeing. In fact, those I engaged with in the mountain regions had an excellent knowledge of the curative properties of local herbs. I was often presented with a flower or leaf, and told, "This will be good for you."

I found that seemingly small things, such as the preparation for a long journey, or scheduling time for rest and relaxation, were very important to the Bulgarians I met. They seemed to take more time for everything and appreciate such things. As well as being knowledgeable about healing methods, massage is practised naturally by most. In fact, if you are visiting the house of a Bulgarian, do not be surprised when, after announcing that you have a sore neck or muscle problem, that your host offers a massage. The people I met seemed to have the ability to know how you are feeling, almost before you do. So many times I was told to relax and take it easy when in Bulgaria, and the country has taught me to appreciate the good things in life—which is always good for the health. These include exercise, meditation, rest, clear water, herbal tea, and the benefits to be had from the pure joy of nature. Of course, we should remember that these are not unique to Bulgaria; there are gifts on offer in whatever part of the world we find ourselves—we just need to seek these out and learn to appreciate them.

A Bulgarian Mystic, photograph by the author

CHAPTER 10

COMMUNING WITH NATURE

I have always been close to nature. Once, when I was walking in the woods I opened my heart to all messages, asked for the light to enter and invited nature to walk with me. It certainly did, as a short time later, a white butterfly flew onto my path. I acknowledged it and for a while the creature flew alongside me as I walked. As it retreated, I heard a voice telling me that I no longer needed to see the butterfly, but that it was a sign that an angel was now with me. I continued walking, comforted by this knowledge, to an ancient fort I knew of, further into the forest.

When I arrived, I saw four wild deer, simply standing there as if they had been waiting on me. They did not run away, but stood watching from a short distance. I moved on towards an ancient oak in the middle of the ruins of the fort and discovered once again, slightly hidden beneath a tree, the same four deer. They had accompanied me to the spot; I felt that this was the spirit of nature confirming its presence. After the deer had gone on their way, I received a message to look at my angel cards, which I did. The advice was to always be open to nature's messages.

*Photograph of a miniature fairy forest near the author's home
to commemorate Erica, a little nine-year-old girl who passed
away, who had always been fascinated by fairies*

This prompted me to think of some advice I'd read on a fairyologist course; it suggested that, if troubled, we should bathe outdoors and release our worries to the water. I immediately felt compelled to go to a nearby lake in order to swim. This presented a minor challenge, as I had no swimming trunks with me. However, I walked on through the thick forest until I found the lake. On the bank, I simply stripped off my clothes and, with great faith, dived in. It really worked and I emerged feeling totally renewed and refreshed.

I walked back through the forest and, on returning to my car, spotted a little bird that was obviously injured and unable to fly. I carefully picked it up and took it home with me. I had just reread a section of *Love Never Dies*, in which the author Dr. Jamie Turndorf describes how those who have passed over sometimes use animals and birds to communicate with the living.

Although, sadly, my little bird friend died, directly afterwards I started to receive messages about canaries. These suggested that, since I already possessed an empty birdcage, I should get one of these birds. I did so, and that canary sang so sweetly to us every day, filling the house with its cheerful sound.

An evening swim in a local lake, taken by the author

I enjoy watching animals and birds immensely, and one day I was admiring a group of swans that often fly directly up the river that runs in front of my house. However, this time they completely changed direction, flew over my head, then turned again and continued on their normal route. At that moment, I felt a real sense of communion with nature and support from the universe.

I have had many other experiences where animals, including foxes, deer and birds have come very close to me, seemingly content to just watch and share their space with me. Once, when I was walking in the forest, a group of swans were swimming out on the lake. When they spotted me, they came over and proceeded to perform what looked like a "guard of honour" as they swam past. They then stopped swimming and remained alongside me for some time.

Although I live in the real world, moments such as these reassure me that I am completely supported by the universe and my ancestors. I really believe that the more we encounter nature and relate to it, the more support and insight we receive.

Spying in Bulgaria

On one of my many trips to Bulgaria, I met a lady whose family had been involved in the production of yoghurt for many years. As Bulgaria is widely considered "the home of yoghurt", I became interested in production techniques, having had the idea that I might introduce its famous technology to Ireland and the UK.

As this lady told me how her father had been instrumental in the development of the yoghurt-making process in the country, I could see that she was becoming increasingly emotional. She revealed that he had committed suicide during the communist era. It turned out that he had been a diplomat attached to overseas embassies for the regime, a privileged position at that time. It enabled his family to live in several European countries, including France and the UK, as well as in the US.

The woman confided that her father had also been a spy for his country, and referred to the infamous British spy, Guy Burgess, who had later defected as a double agent to the then Soviet Union. She remembered Burgess having visited their house on many occasions, and intimated that her father may have also have been a double agent. She concluded by stating that it had never become clear why he had taken his own life. Sometime after this, Bulgaria cast off its communist past and became a democracy; her father's loss of life had served no purpose.

Her story reinforced my conclusions regarding the futility of suicide.

Giving and receiving

I found the following quote from Louise L. Hay's book *You Can Heal Your Life* very inspiring.

> "If we want a joyous life, we must think joyous thoughts.
> If we want a prosperous life, we must think prosperous

thoughts. If we want a loving life, we must think loving thoughts. Whatever we sent out mentally or verbally will come back to us in like form."

It is all too easy to underestimate our capacity for love and the effect that this can have on our fellow humans. While working as a professional photographer, I enjoyed the privilege of being close to clients and their family circle while recording their special events and celebrations. I experienced so much love from ordinary people on extraordinary days, as they celebrated their weddings, christenings, anniversaries and other joyful occasions. I came to the conclusion that it is impossible to truly imagine the extent to which we can make a difference in the world.

However, this message has been communicated many times by those who have experienced the high spiritual realm of the universe through near-death experiences and other communications.

Jesus said that we can do what he did, and more.

I used to judge photographic competitions on a regular basis, both as a practicing professional and after I started teaching photography part-time at a local university. When addressing students, I often quoted an inspirational statement from an American photographer and, in fact, I continue to repeat it in my motivational talks to this day.

> "We are only limited by our imagination, but our imagination has no limits."

Another important quote from Louise L. Hay in *You Can Heal Your Life* is...

> "When we create peace and harmony and balance in our minds, we will find it in our lives."

These are wise words and I have come to realise that this statement applies to all of us in our lives. In being our authentic selves, bringing love to others and acting through love, we can have a massive impact on our families, our communities and, ultimately, our world.

I must admit that I have failed to practice this myself many times, but when I have done, it has led to a sense of fulfilment and knowledge that I have returned to the right path. We should not chastise ourselves too harshly when we fail along the way, as this is just a temporary "glitch." It is much more important to recognise it as such and to learn from the experience and, if necessary, ask for support. This support will always be there whether through our higher self, our angels, or the universe or God (however this is described by your culture, religion or personal belief.)

During an interview the year before he died, I heard Dr. Wayne Dyer highly recommending the book, *The Impersonal Life.* It had originally been published under the pen name, "Anonymous" in the early twentieth century. The author's real name, Joseph Benner, only become known after his death in 1938. He is reported to have chosen anonymity because he was a clergyman who did not want to be identified, as his writings were not in line with his church at the turn of the century. Later, after his death, his wife identified him. In his writings, he expressed the New Thought concept that we are all one with God and that God endows us with the power to create our experiences and reality.

Benner's message is very profound, speaking of man's oneness and the divinity that resides in all of us. While I was endeavouring to understand the complex content of *The Impersonal Life*, I received a text on my phone telling me a new podcast had just been shared online. Something told me that I must listen to it, so I opened the podcast, to discover it was an interview with psychic medium and author, Karen Noé, and Joules Johnston from Law of Attraction Radio. Karen said that she had been receiving messages from Dr. Wayne Dyer from the other side that were directed towards his wife and family. I couldn't believe it when they went on to discuss the book that I was holding in my hands at that precise moment. Karen Noé began to explain Wayne's messages in the book, which greatly helped me to gain an understanding of its contents, proving to me that I was being guided from outside. This was a great relief at a time when I had been criminalised both through peoples' opinion and by attempts to legally "bring me to justice." After this experience, I was reassured that it was what I felt in my heart that was most important: that I was intrinsically good and loving on a higher level. And we all capable of this.

Finding positive from negative

On November 14th, 2016, I left everything behind me in Courtroom 14, High Court, Dublin, when I was adjudicated on my bankruptcy case. The thought of this process would have horrified me in the past, but as a result of the support from family, friends and the universe, I ended up seeking this closure. In fact, I found myself confident enough to complete the entire process alone, without even the assistance of an accountant. This had such a positive effect on me, mentally, that the whole experience ended up being incredibly liberating.

I also discovered that there was something else special happening on the day of my case; a supermoon. This phenomenon occurs when the full moon is at its closest to the earth and on that particular date it was considered extra-special, since it was the largest supermoon since 1948. I was born in 1949, but had been conceived in 1948, and I certainly felt a new light within me. Considered to be a powerful time of release and transformation, this appearance of this supermoon certainly represented this for me. Suddenly, I was back in control of my life and, even though the process had been both daunting and challenging, I had successfully managed to navigate the process of bankruptcy on my own.

This solidly reinforced the truth that I, and therefore anyone, can achieve so much more than can ever be imagined. The following two quotes perfectly sum up my thoughts on this matter. The first is from Mike Dooley's book, *Life on Earth*:

> "We're talking about you living your bliss, and doing so by actively facing your fears, dealing with your challenges, putting out your fires, taking action even when you're lost, and thereby becoming more than you know is possible."

The second quote is from the inspirational Dr. Wayne Dyer:

> "There is one grand lie – that we are limited. The only limits we have are the limits we believe."

Healing hands

Photograph of a tortoiseshell butterfly taken by the author

I believe that we all have healing power, and not just from within; I have discovered that mine come through me from Jesus, Mary and the universe. I have always been told that I had healing powers, as did my father, James. I remember when people from the area used to come to our house for various "cures" for their ailments. These cures were descended from ancient Irish traditions and prayers that had been handed down for generations.

I was told by a medium many years ago that I had this healing power that came from Jesus, through my hands. The first thing that she pointed out to me was that I was a healer, and that this would play an important part of my life. This was confirmed by several other mediums I visited over the years who told me that the gift had been passed down to me by my father. But this "gift" is a skill that I believe everyone possesses, to some extent.

"Let your light shine through" photograph by the author

"Be yourself and let your light shine through"

Young Americans is a group of talented US performers with a mission to encourage young people across the world attain self-confidence, self-esteem and respect for others through music, dance, and performance.

The group visits Ireland each year, touring schools and helping to organise shows in which local students are invited to participate. The programme helps these young people to believe in themselves and develop formerly unknown talents, and is an uplifting experience for the students and their families alike.

I attended one of these performances and while the principal of a college was thanking the *Young Americans* for their great work, she referred to the quote, "Be yourself and let your light shine through." The principal explained that she had overhead one of the American mentors say this to a student, and I believe that this is one of the most important pieces of advice any of us can receive.

Evening light photographed by the author at his house.

Letting go of fear and learning to heal

In October 2016, my good friend Una highly recommended a particular medium/healer named Martin Fall. She said that she'd had some amazing results after a visit. So I simply had to meet this person.

I must admit, after visiting Martin, my faith in myself was restored and he inspired me to continue on my new journey of healing others. He was the most amazing and unusual healer I have ever visited, with healing and psychic abilities rooted in ancient Ireland. When I entered the purpose-built room at the front of his house, I saw that it was filled with traditional artefacts, such as old bicycles and other paraphernalia. Martin was sitting with his shoes off, warming his feet at a turf fire, the traditional method of heating an Irish home in the past.

He didn't say much at first, but "read" me immediately. He told me that I was still living in fear, explaining that this was not fear of the future, but about undertaking what I was destined to do—to heal others. He said that he could see that this was a very strong calling for me, and that I should simply begin my work. According to Martin, I was underestimating myself and my abilities-- even my photography skills! He told me I was too trusting of certain people around me, and that this was the reason that I had experienced such difficulties in my business life. When he added that these problems were not my fault, it was an incredible relief since, despite having entire confidence in my motivations, I continued to have deep feelings of guilt and inadequacy. I know that this sounds contradictory, but it is the only way I can describe my emotions.

Martin then declared that he would take away my fear. To do this, he used an ancient Irish method that employed symbolism. He produced a pebble which he said should be placed under my pillow for ten nights, then instructed me to throw it into a running stream on the tenth day. He also instructed me to scribble freely in a notebook each morning for nine days, but without trying to guide the writing. After nine days, I was to burn the book.

Photograph of a flowing stream taken by the author.
Its water took his fears away.

I did everything as requested and was emotionally quite disturbed on the ninth day. However, on the tenth day I felt totally renewed. I had come a long way in order to let go of my fears—fears of what might happen in the future and fears of beginning my new life of bringing healing to my fellow human beings.

I have now had a chance to absorb all this and am excited about the future, eager to draw upon my life experience for the good of many. So I intend to end my days here on earth fulfilling my destiny to its fullest potential.

My sincere hope is that this book will have inspired you, and that it will encourage you to achieve your own potential in the fullest of ways. From the bottom of my heart, I send you all the blessings of the universe and ask that they accompany you on your journey, wherever it may take you.

EPILOGUE

The words of this song, written by Bob Thiele and made famous by Louis Armstrong, have often inspired me and say such a lot.

What a Wonderful World

I see trees of green, red roses too
I see them bloom for me and you
And I think to myself, what a wonderful world

I see skies of blue and clouds of white
The bright blessed day, the dark sacred night
And I think to myself what a wonderful world

The colors of the rainbow so pretty in the sky
Are also on the faces of people walking by
I see friends shaking hands saying how do you do
They're really saying I love you

Sean Boylan, author of this book, would be delighted to hear from you, now that you have read *A Spiritual Journey*.

To contact Sean, please send an email to seanboylan1528@gmail.com
Or contact him through his websites:
https://www.seanboylan.ie/book/
and
https://seanboylan.simdif.com

Sean Boylan Youtube Law Of Attraction Radio interview
https://www.youtube.com/watch?v=d4Akmj93aNc